PARADISE

PARADISE

Portraying the New Guinea Highlands

Michael O'Hanlon

Published by British Museum Press
for the Trustees of the British Museum

The Trustees of the British Museum gratefully acknowledge the support and encouragement given to its work in Papua New Guinea by The British Museum Society.

Front cover: Kulka Kokn in ceremonial wig. Traditional in form, such wigs are today made from imported materials.

Back cover: The image of Papua New Guinea as paradise is embodied in a netbag and offered for sale to visitors.

Frontispiece: Zacharias (left) and Wik (right) calculate the distribution of pork at the author's leaving party.

Published by British Museum Press
A division of British Museum Publications Ltd
46 Bloomsbury Street
London WC1B 3QQ

British Library Cataloguing in Publication Data
A Catalogue record of this book is available from the British Library

ISBN 0 7141 2509 1

Designed by Behram Kapadia
Drawings by Rebecca Jewell
Maps by Jim Farrant
Printed by BAS Printers Ltd, Over Wallop, Hampshire

Contents

Acknowledgements

Completing this book, and making the collecting trips it describes, have incurred debts in many places. I should like to thank more of my colleagues in the British Museum than I can possibly name here; I cannot, however, pass on without mentioning Ben Burt, Brian Durrans, Margaret Hall, Jill Hasell, Morven Leese, John Mack, Michael Row and Shelagh Weir.

Beyond the Museum, I must thank in particular Rebecca Jewell for her line drawings, and Coryn Greatorex-Bell and Susanna Kelly for their background research. Jonathan Benthall, Paula Brown, James Carrier, Jeremy Coote, Eric Hirsch, Miriam Kahn, Noble Frankland, Rosemary O'Hanlon, Susan Pearce, Tony Shelton, Andrew Strathern and Gabriele Stürzenhofecker suggested many improvements to the manuscript which also greatly benefited from the supportive editorial work of Carolyn Jones of British Museum Press. Mrs Jeanette Leahy most kindly gave me permission to reproduce her husband's unique photographs, and Margaret Taylor also allowed me to consult her father's photograph album. The National Library of Australia, where both sets of photographs are stored, have patiently dealt with my requests for information over the years. John Muke generously shared his own findings on Wahgi shields while Marie Reay and Father Louis Luzbetak, the doyens of Wahgi research, also kindly furnished information on specific points. Remaining defects are mine alone.

The fieldwork on which this study is based was initially funded by the then SSRC and the Leverhulme Trust, and latterly by the Trustees of the British Museum whose support for field research has helped to sustain the relationship which this book describes. I am most grateful to these bodies, but also to the relevant Papua New Guinean authorities for fieldwork permission, and in particular to Soroi Eoe and Pam Swadling at the National Museum to which I was affiliated. The collection on which the exhibition is based was funded by the British Museum Society, to whom go my special thanks.

At various times, Christine Bradley, Graham Richmond, and John and Racheal Burton generously housed my wife Linda and me while we completed necessary formalities in Papua New Guinea's capital, Port Moresby. However, it is in the New Guinea Highlands that I accumulated the greatest range of debts. Yimbal Aipe and Tai unhesitatingly allowed me to draw upon the takings of their trade-stores to avoid having to transport cash along the Highlands Highway too often; Bob Connolly and Robin Anderson shared their own Highlands experience and rendered other practical assistance; Inspector Manguva and Corporal Pakyo made available a number of captured shields and rifles for inspection; Michael Du made the crates in which the collection travelled, while the shield-decorator Kaipel Ka addressed them and has also patiently answered my questions since then. Philip Kapal, Mark Wom, John Kandil, Joe and Josephine Goi, Paple Kerenga, Kulam, Opuns, Irene Munum, Kauwiye and Kaunga Aipe and the staff of Fatima School were amongst the many who also gave information and practical assistance.

Actually making the collection would have been quite impossible without the daily help of Wik, Ngunz, Pilo, Munumb, Bruce, Ak, Nosa, Tongl, Gun, Alu and others who were also companions and minders. As always, my major thanks in the Wahgi must go to those of Topkalap settlement, and in particular to the sisters Ner and Dir, to Kos and Waiang, but most of all to Zacharias, Bruce, Paiye, and to my sponsor Kinden. And as always, whether in the Wahgi or elsewhere, I owe the greatest debt to my wife, Linda.

Introduction

This book is written to accompany **Paradise**, an exhibition at the Museum of Mankind (the Ethnography Department of the British Museum), dealing with the culture and history of the Wahgi people of the Papua New Guinea Highlands (see map 1). While I hope the book fulfils the standard functions of an exhibition catalogue – to provide information additional to that given in the exhibition, and in more durable and portable form – it also has a further purpose, one stemming in part from my own earlier involvement with the Wahgi.

Well before I became a museum curator, I had spent two years (1979-81) doing anthropological fieldwork in the northwest Wahgi area. There my wife and I had lived on the east bank of the Kar River amongst Komblo tribe (map 2), one of whose prominent men, Kinden of Kekanem clan, was our main sponsor in the society. Partly for historical reasons – Papua New Guinea was administered by Australia until it became an independent state in 1975 – the material culture of the New Guinea Highlands is not well represented in the British Museum's collections. When I subsequently joined the staff of the museum, the combination of this gap in the collections and the links which I had maintained with Kinden and other Wahgi, suggested an opportunity to develop this area of the museum's work. With a view to adding contemporary Wahgi material to the collections, for ultimate use in an exhibition, I made a three-month collecting trip back to the same community on the Kar River in 1986 and again in 1990.

Because I was collecting artefacts in a community which I knew quite well, I was able to document the items I was collecting in greater detail than is often possible for museum collections. This was less a technical matter of observing how particular artefacts are made. It was more a question of using the extensive genealogies compiled during my earlier fieldwork to place who had originally made the artefacts and when; and to whom (in a society in which much of politics revolves around the exchange of material objects) the artefact had then been given and why. I found that I could use my knowledge of the community to give the artefacts I collected something of an individual biography, rather than treating them as anonymous types.

I also began to find that the activity of collecting was informative in itself. The practical engagement with objects provided robust confirmation of information which my more generally-phrased questions as an anthropologist had produced only in tenuous form; occasionally, the process of collecting threw

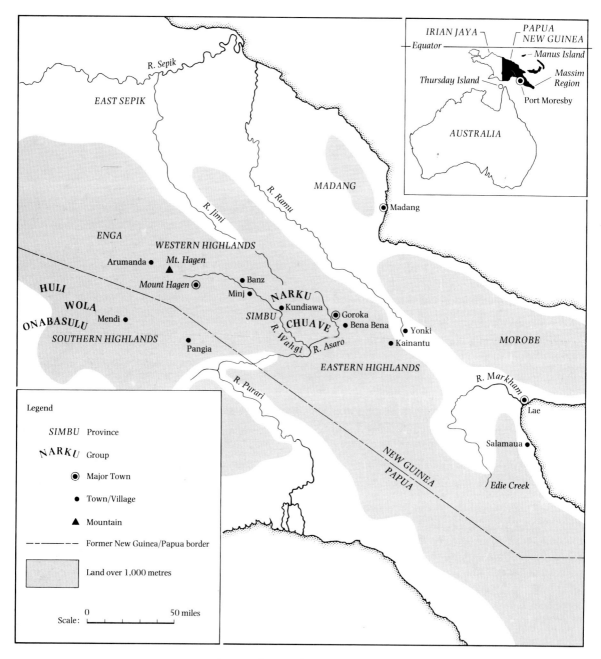

Map 1: Papua New Guinea Highlands.

up entirely new data and perspectives. At the same time, the fact that I was working in a community which I knew well made me more aware of how my collecting activities were seen by the Wahgi. In fact, a few weeks before my visit to the Wahgi in July 1990, a dance troupe from Papua New Guinea had toured Europe, visiting Britain where, amongst other venues, they danced in Acton in West London. The performers had included a group from the Mt. Hagen area, neighbours to the Wahgi in the Western Highlands Province (map 1). On arriving in the Wahgi, I found that news of the Hageners' visit

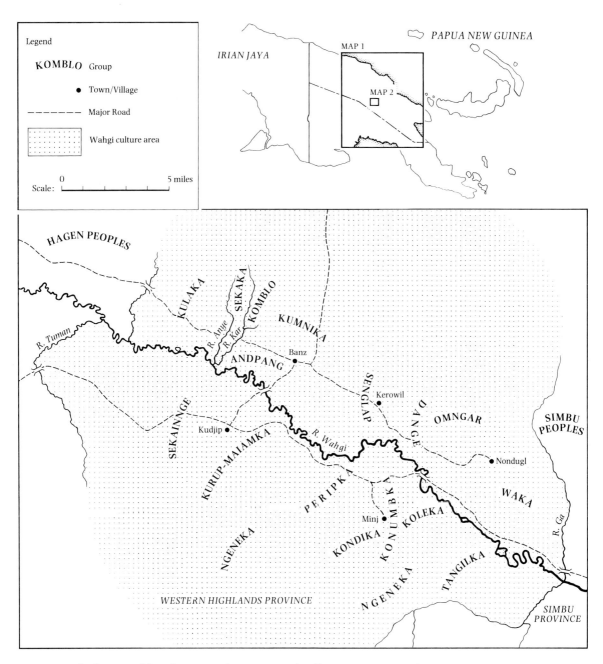

Map 2: Central Wahgi Valley, showing approximate position of groups mentioned in text.

to Britain had created local expectations as to why I was now returning. Equally, the Papua New Guinea dancers' trip to Britain had given me an opportunity to observe something of British spectators' reactions and the way the media portrayed the visitors.

In short, I found that the exhibition which I had planned resisted being confined to the moment of its going on show. My previous residence with the Wahgi conditioned the circumstances under which I made the collection, as did the visit of the Papua New Guinea dancers to Britain. Nor were the

Wahgi themselves passive onlookers in the exercise. They had ideas of their own as to what making a collection of material culture involved, and the process of helping me do so also stimulated them to reflect on cultural changes. Equally, exhibitions themselves do not come ready-made. They involve choices with respect to which curators, designers and others who have the task of realising an exhibition may have different ideas. At a time when funding for exhibitions can be uncertain, the scale and the precise form to be taken by an exhibition may need to be kept flexible until quite close to its opening.

Writing an exhibition catalogue in such circumstances offered the opportunity to incorporate these various complexities, interconnections and uncertainties: to see them not just as technical problems, but as much a part of the data as the information about the exhibits themselves. I therefore hope this book may be of interest to three specialist groups, in addition to a general readership. For the burgeoning number of academic courses on museums, it might serve as a partial ethnography of an exhibition. For anthropologists interested in Melanesia and in material culture, it provides fresh information on contemporary Highlands artefacts and their context. Finally, for my Wahgi hosts of Komblo tribe it is a record of what the influential men, into whose orbits Highlands anthropologists tend to gravitate, felt that it was important for others to know about them and their history. In all cases, an outline of the plan of the book may be helpful.

The first chapter has a number of goals. One is to provide an outline of Wahgi culture, supplying background information on the context from which the artefacts displayed in the exhibition derive. This context is one of momentous change. It is precisely sixty years since the first Whites, members of the Leahy-Taylor patrol, walked into the broad Wahgi Valley, to surprise the world with their descriptions of a large population of stone-using horticulturalists in a region hitherto thought to have been unpopulated. Mick Leahy, joint leader of this expedition in search of gold, happened also to be a talented photographer; his pictures (some of which appear in the exhibition) record one of the last occasions on which really large populations previously unknown to the outside world were encountered, and both parties' reactions to the event.

The ensuing decades saw something of a crash-course in modernity for the Wahgi and neighbouring Highlands peoples. No sooner did the waxing colonial presence begin to suppress local inter-group warfare than the Wahgi were touched by the edge of global conflict, with the outbreak of the Pacific War. This brought in its wake an epidemic of dysentery, a disease new to the Highlands, which resulted in hundreds of deaths. Then the Australian Administration re-established itself after the close of the Pacific War, bringing in its train labour migration, missions and a growing engagement in the world market through the introduction of coffee as a cash crop. With the aid of their new cash income, the Wahgi introduced themselves to a range of manufactured goods which replaced substantial sections of their material culture. The boom in coffee prices in the 1970s then multiplied the Wahgi capacity to import such goods many times over. Tensions over coffee land and income are linked to the renewal of inter-group fighting which preceded Papua New Guinea's political independence in 1975, and which has continued intermittently since.

Only a historical perspective can accommodate such switchback developments, and here I view the Wahgi more generally through sketching the dramatic history of one specific tribe: Komblo, the group with whom I have worked most closely.[1] Komblo's own history underlines a further point: that while the arrival of the Leahy-Taylor patrol certainly marked a watershed, it was in no sense the beginning of recorded time for Highlands peoples. For, like many other Wahgi groups, Komblo are themselves immigrants and have an elaborate oral tradition of how they came to the area, where they first settled, and the other tribes with whom they intermarried. Since it is so important politically, marriage is in fact an excellent framework for exploring Wahgi history. Here I use a chart of the marriages made over the past century by one section of Komblo as a way of highlighting significant stages in their history (see p.24). Komblo's arrival in the Wahgi area and the fluctuations in their relationship with neighbouring tribes are neatly reflected in marriage patterns. These same patterns also show the increasing but distinctly uneven integration of the Wahgi within Papua New Guinea more broadly. They reflect the growing prosperity of the Wahgi in relation to peoples in surrounding provinces, as Wahgi coffee wealth attracts increasing numbers of wives from less developed areas – women who bring with them, for example, new designs and styles of making the netbags which are heavily represented in the exhibition.

However, while outlining the radical changes experienced over these decades, Chapter 1 also brings out the equally striking continuities – and the extent to which 'tradition' and 'change' are not always the mutually exclusive things we sometimes take them to be. It was, for example, the Australian-imposed peace which provided the conditions in which could flourish the elaborate ceremonies which have often made the Wahgi look very 'traditional'; coffee income is used to make compensation payments for battle deaths; and car accidents may be attributed to the anger of ancestral ghosts.

All this is rather at odds with one popular image – indeed, a romantic fear – we have about such peoples as the Wahgi. According to this stereotype, they are 'traditional' until encountered by the West, then become increasingly less so as their local culture is tragically eroded and displaced by imported Western institutions, material values and manufactured goods. The process tends to be imagined as a zero-sum game in which, as the amount of 'change' increases, so the extent of 'tradition' necessarily diminishes. Certainly, such an assumption lies behind many of the enquiries a museum receives. Indeed, to some extent this perspective is built into museums themselves, because if cultures are *not* changing so radically, not always on the point of disappearing, the urgency of collecting and preserving their objects is from one point of view diminished.[2] Yet, as emerges in Chapter 1, to imagine the process purely as one of inexorable extinction of cultural diversity is to overlook the capacity of cultures creatively to select, adapt and re-contextualise external forms. To use Hannerz's (1991) vocabulary, what is going on is not necessarily a process of global 'homogenization', so much as one of 'creolization'.

The second chapter substantiates some of these points through looking at the artefacts themselves. The contemporary shields on display are a good example. They are at once traditional in form and innovative in their materials and decoration, drawing upon such non-indigenous designs as lager advertisements – which may yet be read in traditional Wahgi terms. As Thomas (1991:185-6) has cautioned, 'appearances may be misleading ... introduced artifacts and models of social organization need to be interpreted in the context of the place into which they are introduced, and not taken as essences that have merely been moved physically from places of origin'.

But Chapter 2 also surveys aspects of the process of making the collection on which the exhibition is based. The trend in anthropology over the last decade towards a more subjective style has produced some notable personal accounts of fieldwork : accounts, that is to say, of collecting information. Much less has been written by anthropologists about the process of collecting arte-facts, though many anthropologists make such collections either for museums or for themselves, or are presented with artefacts as part of their interaction with their hosts. This chapter is intended to add to the small corpus of writing on the topic.

One reason for anthropologists' reticence in describing the process of mak-ing collections may be that the whole idea of accumulating assemblages of artefacts from other cultures has recently come to be viewed with considerable reserve. Stewart (1984:153) has voiced one concern: that when an artefact is incorporated into a collection its new status as representing that *type* of artefact supplants its original context. As she puts it, 'the collection replaces origin with classification'. A second concern, of course, has been the colonial background to much collecting. Another has to do with the politics of repre-sentation : the possessors of such collections have used them to create images of the cultures from which the artefacts come, images over which the people represented exercise no control. Historically, such images have often proved to have more to do with the preoccupations of those doing the representing than those being represented – the way in which the media portrayed the visit of the Highlands dancers to Britain was one spectacular example of this (see Chapter 2).

Clifford has done more than most to articulate the disquiet which issues of collecting artefacts and representing cultures have raised. Asking where such artefacts truly belong, he says (1985:244) 'I have been suggesting that they "belong" nowhere, having been torn from their social contexts of produc-tion and reception, given value in systems of meaning whose primary function is to confirm the knowledge and taste of a possessive Western subjectivity'. But it seems to me important that in our efforts to acknowledge this where it is so, we do not inadvertently swamp rather different local perceptions as to what might be going on in specific cases. In societies such as those of the New Guinea Highlands, in which much of politics revolves around the accumulation of objects and their presentation to other groups, collecting may be interpreted rather differently. If we are becoming conditioned to view ethno-graphic collections as cultural hostages, their producers may choose to repre-sent them as envoys in a continuing relationship.[3]

There is a further risk that, preoccupied with our own active role in acquisi-tion (the 'tearing' of objects from their contexts to which Clifford refers), we may overlook the extent to which collecting as a process is also constrained, and collections may carry in themselves a hidden indigenous order. A dominant theme in Wahgi society, for example, is the tension between the allegiance that a man owes his own clan as against that felt to be due to his 'source people' (the clan from which his mother came, and, more remotely, the clans from which his father's mother, mother's mother etc. derive). Both these frameworks, and the tension between them, proved to influence the terms under which I was able to make a collection, and the collection itself partly reflected these local principles in ways I later explain. In short, we must ensure that in our efforts to rectify earlier failings we do not impose a fresh subjugation by ignoring local agency and perceptions.

The brief third chapter describes some of the processes and constraints involved in putting the Wahgi artefacts on exhibition. Partly, this is an attempt to carry forward the point broached in the preceding chapter: that exhibiting, like collecting, takes place within a context which affects the outcome. Just as local Wahgi frameworks proved to guide the making of the collection, so the museum setting to which the artefacts were subsequently brought has its own history and constraints. These inevitably influence how Wahgi culture will 'look' when it is exhibited. I therefore devote to the artefacts' new ethnographic context of Mayfair galleries a measure of the same attention earlier paid to their Wahgi setting. However, because this final chapter is necessarily written well before the opening date of the exhibition, when most of the design and other work remains to be done, it is unavoidably incomplete. Nor can it take fully into account the profusion of writing on exhibitions and on representation which has been published just within the last year or two. Nevertheless, such literature does not generally deal with instances in which the exhibitor has had the fortune to work in the field, to make the collection, and to be involved in exhibiting it. In these circumstances it seems worth sketching, however incompletely, some of the background to the display itself, and in this way rounding off a brief ethnography of an exhibition.

A brief note on Papua New Guinea's geographical and political circumstances, and on the conventions adopted in this book, may be useful here. Papua New Guinea comprises the eastern half of the island of New Guinea – the western section being Irian Jaya, part of Indonesia. Papua New Guinea's capital is Port Moresby; its currency is the Kina whose value, over the last decade, has averaged around K1.5 to £1 sterling. In addition to these terms the names of a considerable number of Wahgi groups and subgroups are unavoidably, and intentionally, introduced: it is impossible to convey anything of the specifics or the feel of the history recounted in Chapter 1 without doing so. Readers will encounter not only Komblo and its neighbouring tribes whose location is shown in map 2, but also the major Komblo subgroups: Kulka, Jiruka and Ngunzka – the last of which split into the separate clans of Kekanem and Anzkanem in the tragic circumstances described. Membership of such groups is to a considerable extent the basis of the social identity of Wahgi individuals, including those whose names I have equally deliberately incorporated in this account. Indeed, in the case of men, Wahgi sometimes prefix an individual's name with that of his group. This is a practice which I adopt here in those instances in which an individual's group membership is relevant to the matter in hand: thus my sponsor Kinden might be referred to as Komblo Kinden, to denote his membership of Komblo tribe. The names both of groups and of individuals have, of course, been suppressed or changed where I felt that publication might break a confidence.

CHAPTER ONE

The Wahgi: change and continuity in Highland New Guinea

Social geography

Stretching westward from what is today Simbu Province (map 1), the Wahgi Valley gradually broadens until it spills out against the base of Mount Hagen some sixty miles away. Fast streams run down from the valley walls, which in places rise to heights over 4,000 metres, to join the meandering Wahgi River as it flows eastward. For the Wahgi people, today numbering 75,000 or so, who inhabit the central section of the valley (map 2), this spectacular geography of valley walls and river provides a spatial frame-work in terms of which they orient all their activities. In 'real talk' (as the Wahgi call their language), places and events are generally referred to by expressions which locate them as up- or down-river from the speaker, as towards the river, away from it, or across it; as on higher or lower ground.[1] These precise orienting terms are used even within the house, so that someone who spots an item for which another is searching may direct them to it by saying, for example, 'it's just "up-river"'. In contrast, far distant places (to which Wahgi business men and women and politicians now regularly travel) are all classified as lying in the same direction: Port Moresby, Sydney, and New York are all described as 'down-river and below'.

Since even the valley floor is 1,600 metres above sea level, the temperature is relatively cool and varies little throughout the year. Rainfall is, however, heavy (180-250 cm a year), December to May being the generally wetter months. The Wahgi calculate their own calendar from shifts in the point at which the sun rises, and relate these to wetter and drier times, and to such processes as the swelling and ripening of pandanus nuts and fruit, products which Wahgi clans exchange with each other. A myth in fact relates the Wahgi calendar (which they call *anz kamben to*) to a cosmic exchange cycle between a northern star, Kopn Moru, and a southern one, Boma Walep. As the sun's point of rising swings towards the south ('down towards' then 'across' the Wahgi river, from the point of view of a tribe like Komblo to the river's north), it is said to be carrying pandanus oil and *mormi*, the iridescent beetle shells used in decorative headbands (fig. 1), from Kopn Moru to Boma Walep.[2] Then, as the sun's point of rising swings back again over the course of the year, it is said to be bringing gifts of pork and wing-beans back from Boma Walep to Kopn Moru. At its most expansive, the myth ties into the calendar not only the times at which pigs fatten, and the frightening periods known as *goli tom*, in which people seem to die one after another, but even

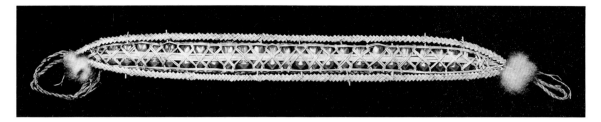

Fig. 1 Headband of green beetle carapaces (*mormi*) in golden cane lattice; tuft of marsupial fur at either end. 1990 Oc.9.523; L: 71.3 cm.

earthquakes and thunder (both said to be caused by the sun standing up and shaking itself, before moving off from the 'house' of one of the stars to that of its exchange partner).

New Guinea Highland societies have often been described as exhibiting 'unity in diversity', and in many ways the Wahgi are typical of the dense populations of this area of the Highlands. They are horticulturalists, growing sweet potato as the staple food both for people and for the herds of pigs they raise. The people live not in villages, but in smaller settlements scattered over the foothills, preferring to avoid both the swampy valley floor and the cloudy heights of the valley walls. As elsewhere in the Highlands, there is a marked division of labour, with men doing the heavier, intermittent work of house, fence and garden-making, while women have day-to-day care of pigs and gardens. And like other Pacific peoples, the Wahgi had a neolithic technology until contact with outsiders: in fact the stone axe mines on the Tuman River, towards the western end of the valley, supplied much of the Highlands with high-quality blades (Burton 1984:4-5).

Politically, the Wahgi are organised in localised clans (generally numbering a few hundred people) which in turn generally belong to larger tribes. Groups at both these levels make use of a patrilineal ideology both in accounting for their internal structure (for example, explaining a clan's subgroups as each founded by one of a set of brothers), and in appealing for internal unity and cooperation. As elsewhere in the Highlands, inter-group relations are traditionally conducted in the idiom of exchange. Such life-cycle events as marriage and death involve the exchange of valuables – in the past, items like marsupial jawbones (fig. 2), axes and the few shell ornaments which were traded up from the coast; today, pigs and cash. Wahgi clans are exogamous, and marriage itself is often seen as an exchange of women between the clans involved, sometimes taking the form of true sister-exchange. Deaths in inter-group warfare may also be expressed as a kind of exchange: 'we have exchanged deaths, both are equal', people may say. Wahgi groups are led not by hereditary chiefs but by 'big' or 'great' men: prominent individuals who organise and dominate these exchanges by means of their forceful personalities, oratorical powers, manipulation of the networks along which valuables flow, and use of the labour of their wives and of younger men.

Yet if in these respects Wahgi society exhibits 'unity' with surrounding cultures, it also seems set off from them in its unusually deep concern with clan solidarity on the one hand and loyalties owed outside the clan on the other. Anthropologists have sometimes found it fruitful to think of Highlands societies as arising from the interplay of opposing principles of one kind and another, and much of Wahgi life can be seen in terms of this particular tension. Certainly, the importance of clan unity, strength and numbers are themes

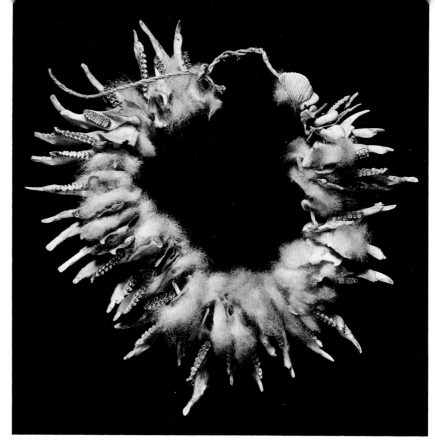

Fig. 2 Necklace of marsupial jawbones, fur and small shells. 1990 0c.9.605; DIA: 21 cm.

which are often voiced in the lead-up to such events as the Pig Festival, which is performed once every twenty years or so and is intended to appease the collectivity of clan ghosts and to overwhelm spectators with the power and beauty of the accompanying dancing. A jealous regard for clan strength is also evidenced both in the way men may compare the number of brides they have sent to swell the size of other clans with those received in return, and in Wahgi marriage rules, which enjoin a set of brothers to offer a girl in marriage to the group which provided their mother.

This concern with clan solidarity and strength is further manifested in the fear that these very qualities may be undermined from within. Wahgi worry intermittently that witches and poisoners may be secretly at work within the clan, or that a slighted member may covertly deliver some token, such as a cigarette butt, to an enemy group. The recipients of such a clandestine gift will bury it under a hardwood stake, shavings from which they will use in any subsequent fighting against the donors. It is thought that the betrayed man will inevitably be killed in such fighting. However, the entire clan is also felt to be at long-term risk, since the ghost of the betrayed individual is thought likely to visit sickness, infertility and death upon his whole group while they harbour the traitor. Only through exposing the originating act of betrayal, and instituting food taboos to separate the families of victim and accused, can the debilitating spiral be checked. Consequently, notions of hidden anger, concealed grudges and confession are salient aspects of Wahgi culture.

All these beliefs privilege the clan into which men are born, and to which women move in marriage, as the crucial unit which must guard its strength against external opponents and internal traitors. Yet, as individuals, people are *also* felt to owe loyalties outside the clan, to the clans from which their mothers came and, more remotely, to those from which their fathers' mothers and mothers' mothers came. All these external groups are spoken of as an individual's 'sources', felt to exercise a continuing influence over that individual, just as the head of a stream influences what goes on down-river. In return, individuals are expected to make payments to their immediate 'source people', generally to their mothers' brothers, whose displeasure is otherwise thought capable of bringing down misfortune on neglectful sisters' children. A sister's child, for example, must take great care never to handle any sorcerous token which he suspects may have been given his own clan for use against that of his mother's relatives.

Because Wahgi clans tend to intermarry repeatedly over the generations, the supposedly unified clan is likely to contain a number of blocks, each composed of people 'born of women' (amb kusil) from a limited number of other clans. These 'shadow communities'[3] within the clan may compete with each other: for example, to champion an incoming bride from their own common 'source' clan as against a girl from another. Each such 'shadow community' is itself internally divided, and in fact replicates the relationship with 'source' people outside the clan. This is because the first girl to marry into a clan from a given other group is thought of as the enabling 'path' along which all other girls marrying in from that same group must travel. She and her descendants are thus the 'sources' for them and their descendants, and exercise the same powers over them as do their respective maternal kin outside the clan. But despite being internally divided in this way, members of 'shadow communities' within a clan can at times operate as powerful forces opposing the interests of the clan more generally. Ideally, intermarried clans should not engage in warfare against each other but when they do so, these external loyalties are revealed as lines of fissure along which individuals defect and clans may fragment.

The return of the dead

At the end of the 1920s, however, the Australians who ruled the then Mandated Territory of New Guinea did not appreciate that the mountainous interior of the island concealed great valleys and complex cultures. Then, in 1926, a gold strike at Edie Creek brought to New Guinea a rush of Australian miners who, once the profitable claims had been staked or exhausted, began to push westward into the Highlands proper.

Prominent among the prospectors was the remarkable Mick Leahy, one of four brothers who were to spend much of their lives in New Guinea. Illness, and a lack of resources with which to exploit his claim, lost Leahy a fortune at Edie Creek. In the years that followed he attempted to remedy this through a series of arduous prospecting journeys which, by 1932, had disclosed the Asaro and Bena Bena Valleys at the eastern end of the Highlands (map 1), and led him to suspect the existence of further valleys and populations to the west. By this point, Leahy, as a tried prospector yet with few resources of his own, was backed by the New Guinea Goldfields Company (NGG) for whom the recent rise in the price of gold made the discovery of fresh prospecting grounds particularly attractive. A secret flight from Bena Bena on 8 March 1933, financed by NGG, confirmed both the existence of a great valley to the west and the joint determination of Leahy and his backers to get there before their commercial rivals.

Such freelance prospecting posed a dilemma for the Australian Administration. On the one hand, it was regarded as an irregular way of bringing into official ambit what were classified as 'uncontrolled areas'. On the other, the process was a difficult one to halt and further gold strikes promised a source of revenue. James Taylor, the Administration's representative on the spot, was told of the planned expedition and made hasty arrangements to accompany it as joint leader with Leahy. The White personnel of the expedition – Mick Leahy, his brother Dan, Taylor and the NGG's surveyor Spinks – then made a further flight over the area to reconnoitre their planned route. Partly in response to the precipitous terrain, air transport had developed very early in New Guinea, and aircraft were to be in use throughout the months of the expedition. 'We were now in the unique position', wrote Taylor (1933a:2) in the resumé to his impressive official report on the patrol, 'of having seen from the air the country we were to examine on foot'.

Crucially, the dense populations disclosed by the flight meant that bulky foodstuffs with which to feed the expedition's carriers could be dispensed with. Instead, the means to buy food *en route* – trade goods and particularly shell – could be taken: 'this enabled us to use the line of porters for the carriage of equipment which otherwise could not have been taken' (*op. cit.*:2). Among this equipment was Mick Leahy's 16mm movie camera, and one of the new lightweight 35 mm Leica cameras which, along with fast and reliable Kodak film, had opened new possibilities for rapid, unposed photography. The country through which the patrol was to move contained one of the last great populations to be encountered by the outside world. The combination of Leahy's own abilities as a photographer (he also processed the negatives himself *en route*) and the new technology was to result in some of the most striking pictures of first contact ever taken.[4] On 28 March 1933 the patrol set out from Bena Bena.

As Schieffelin (1991:3) has perceptively remarked with regard to another pathbreaking expedition of the period – the 1935 Hides-O'Malley patrol through Papua which forms an illuminating contrast in many respects with the Leahy-Taylor expedition – such occasions of first contact were encounters between entire cultural systems:

> a very different situation from that in which a single outsider (a shipwrecked sailor, for example) arrives in a place where people have never seen his kind before. In that case, regardless of what cultural wisdom he can bring to bear on the situation, to the local inhabitants he is merely an anomaly who acts in the capacity of an individual.

In contrast, a major patrol embodies in its internal organisation the distinctions and values of a whole society. In addition to the four Whites and the carriers, the Leahy-Taylor expedition included personal servants, seven policemen, two overseers, a medical orderly and a number of young Bena Bena men who had asked to be included: eighty-two in all. The complexity of these overt distinctions and the ritual of patrol arrangements and movement were further grist for the interpretative mills of the Wahgi and other peoples who were to encounter the expedition.

As the patrol moved westward through the peoples of what is today recognised as Simbu Province, the crowds of curious Highlanders who accompanied it to the edge of their respective territories posed an acute security worry for the expedition leaders. Police were distributed along the length of the line of march, and though the patrol was soon among language groups with whom they could only communicate through signs, they managed to insist that all bows should be carried unstrung. Every afternoon, when camp was made, a rope carried for the purpose was used to mark a boundary (clearly visible in Leahy's photographs) beyond which Highlanders were not permitted to approach. The power of the firearms carried by the patrol was regularly demonstrated by shooting pigs purchased for food. However, as Taylor described in his report, on its first passage westward the patrol was received almost everywhere without hostility. As I discuss below for the Wahgi, this was because the patrol members were often thought to be of supernatural origin, at times being recognised as relatives returned from the dead.

On 6 April, the patrol crossed the Ga River, the tributary marking the eastern border of the Wahgi culture area (map 2). The local people made an

Fig. 3 Wahgi inspect the intruders at mid-Wahgi camp, April 1933; tent in background. M.J. Leahy Collection, Roll 30 Q/7/27.

immediate impression on the patrol. Taylor, who was himself later to marry a Wahgi girl, wrote in his preliminary report on the patrol (1933b:2) 'here the people . . . are probably one of the finest types in New Guinea and . . . by the uniformity of stature and fine physique look as if they had been bred eugenically . . .'. The men, Taylor recorded, were dressed in wide bark belts from which were suspended aprons (fig. 3). These, like Wahgi head gear, had marsupial fur rolled into the bark fibre from which they were netted. Wrist, ankle and waist bands of cane were also worn, as were conus shell nose ornaments and 'the half-moon shaped gold lip shell . . . a possession connoting great wealth and . . . much sought after by these people' (1933a:45). Both Taylor and Mick Leahy commented particularly upon the long spears, often triple-barbed and decorated with marsupial fur. When the patrol paused the following day to flatten a landing strip for resupply, they forced the thousands of visitors to the camp to park these spears in thickets some distance away (fig. 4). While the patrol rested for a few days here in the territory of Senglap tribe, the Wahgi had their best opportunity to inspect the intruders, as the plane brought in new supplies of trade goods along with the NGG's geologist, who reported the area to be unpromising for gold (fig. 5).

In coming to terms with an event such as the arrival of the patrol, people inevitably draw upon their existing cultural categories. A coincidental fit between a particular category and the intruders may structure the way in which the parties interact, with profound consequences for both – as Sahlins (1985) has shown with respect to the Hawaiians' identification of Captain Cook as the god Lono, and their honouring and later killing of him. This liter-

Fig. 4 Wahgi visitors to the patrol's camp were made to park their spears at a distance; James Taylor to right. M.J. Leahy Collection, Roll 81 xviii R/6.

Fig. 5 Wahgi watch from
behind rope barrier at the
airstrip; plane in background.
M.J. Leahy Collection, Roll 81
xviii R/22.

ature on 'first contact' has recently been extended by Schieffelin and Crittenden's exceptional account, referred to above, of the varying reactions of
different Papuan societies to the Hides-O'Malley expedition. Schieffelin and
Crittenden note that the impact made by that patrol varied according to
whether the members happened to be identified with major figures in a local
cosmology, or only with minor beings, and also upon such factors as the direction from which the intruders approached. For example, the direction from
which the Hides-O'Malley expedition approached the territory of the Huli
people (map 1), along with the specifics of local cosmology, led the Huli to
interpret the patrol's arrival as evidence of the deterioration of the world, with
which Huli cosmology is much concerned.

People's experience of first contact also depended upon whether the 'fit'
with local cosmology dictated any action. The Onabasulu, for example, cate-
gorised the few steel axes and bushknives which had earlier found their way
into their territory as items from the Origin Time. News of the approaching
Hides-O'Malley patrol was interpreted as an indication that the 'owners' of
these items were now coming to reclaim them, which was also taken as a
worrying sign of the imminent end of the world. In consequence, some
Onabasulu attempted to hurry the patrol on its way by restituting these items,
and were disconcerted to find that far from carrying the dangerous things
away, Hides and O'Malley left more of them in a doomed effort to establish
good relations.

In the Wahgi instance, while the Leahy-Taylor patrol was generally felt
to be of supernatural origin, there was no precise agreement as to the nature
of the intruders. Many Wahgi did identify them as the dead returning: in fact,
the noise of the plane was often sought for on and in the ground, before it
was spotted in the sky. Other Wahgi focused upon differences amongst the
patrol: the Whites were interpreted as the Sky Being, Seye, sometimes held

to be responsible for thunder and lightning, whilst the police and carriers were identified as Kopo, Seye's black underworld counterpart – both Kopo and Seye being somewhat marginal figures in Wahgi cosmology in comparison to the dead. The light-coloured clothing of the patrol members was also referred to as 'sun garments', and linked to the fact that they approached from the east.

However, this interpretation of the patrol in broadly supernatural terms also had an experimental, matter-of-fact quality to it. It certainly did not mean that the Wahgi shunned the patrol, as the Onabasulu tried to avoid the Hides-O'Malley expedition. Some Wahgi do recall their fear, and others remember how, as children, they were forbidden by their parents to eat morsels of food given them by the patrol ('food of the dead: if you eat it, you'll die!'). The patrol's temporary camp was nevertheless crowded and generally there was a deep interest in, and positive desire to acquire, their artefacts and to incorporate them into indigenous exchanges. Taylor's report does not specify what items were traded on this first encounter. We may assume shell and axes but what Wahgi today particularly recall are such items as the lids from tin cans (fig. 6) which were seized upon and used as alternatives to bailer shell forehead

Fig. 6 Tin lids were amongst the items incorporated in the local decorative repertoire, in place of bailer shell forehead ornaments. M.J. Leahy Collection, Roll 81 xviii R/12.

ornaments. At the same time, the expedition's possession of these material goods was *also* seen as further testament to the members' supernatural origins.

On 14 April, the patrol moved on from Senglap territory, leaving a small contingent on the airstrip under the charge of Buase, one of the accompanying police. The patrol marched along the readily identifiable 'well defined grass covered ridge' (pl. 1) which stretches westward from the present-day town of Banz, before passing out of the Wahgi culture area.

'People from the stony places'

One of the last rivers the patrol crossed that day before leaving the Wahgi culture area was the Kar, which bisected the territory of Komblo tribe. Taylor's report diary notes baldly 'We descended and crossed the Gardnor at 12.50, at 5,333 ft. at water level. Lots of granite and similar rocks were noticed in the stream'.[5] Komblo themselves, however, were not there then, having just been expelled in warfare by an alliance of their neighbours. Many Komblo had in fact sought refuge with Senglap Baiman kin, so had been among those Wahgi to inspect the Leahy-Taylor patrol at the temporary aerodrome a few miles to the east. Since such Komblo describe themselves as only having very recently taken up residence with their Senglap relatives when the patrol arrived, it is likely that their expulsion can be dated to 1931 or 1932.

This, though, was only one of a number of occasions on which Komblo had moved, for they trace their own history much further back, and further to the east, to Narku, a group in what is today Simbu Province (map 1). Although this history is cast in somewhat mythic form, it is almost certainly based on fact (see Brookfield and Brown 1963:87). Simbu more generally seems long to have been a migration source for people travelling westward, and in recounting their own departure, Komblo often mention groups in the Hagen area and in the Jimi Valley who, they say, equally originated in Simbu: indeed migrants continue to take the same route today. Details of Komblo's originating exodus from Simbu vary somewhat with the teller. All agree that there was a theft of *silsalse* eggs which, though of no intrinsic value, are not infrequently cited in Wahgi myth as a cause of dispute. Jiruka and Kulka, two of Komblo's constituent groups, are said to have fled the resulting fighting, escaping down a long tunnel. (Escape tunnels built in the floors of men's houses did in fact exist among some groups in this area; Mick Leahy [1937:166] recorded seeing one in his own narrative of the patrol.) In some accounts, the *silsalse* eggs were stolen specifically by a Jiruka child, the first of many occasions in which Komblo's other constituent groups accuse Jiruka of having initiated conflicts, flights and wars.

Left behind when Jiruka and Kulka fled was the founder of the third main Komblo group, Ngunzka, who is often named as Bombian and said to have been married to a girl from Jiruka or Kulka. According to the myth, this girl, sometimes named as Korkoram, was distressed at her brothers' departure and, with her husband, set out after them. (In other accounts, it is rather Bombian who is presented as upset at the departure of his sister, said to have been married into Jiruka or Kulka; in yet others, Jiruka and Kulka were fleeing from Ngunzka.) Jiruka and Kulka are said to have settled among the powerful Kumnika tribe at Sipil near the present town of Banz, some miles east of their present territory on the Kar River. At Sipil, they were joined by Ngunzka and his wife, who are said to have been delayed *en route* at the swollen Ga River, until they were assisted by the local Waka tribe in building a bridge to cross it. Following further disagreements with their Kumnika hosts at Sipil, the constituent Komblo groups are then said to have moved the few miles further west to the headwaters of the Kar: Ngunzka and Bangkanem, a subgroup of Jiruka, moving first, so getting greater amounts of land.

Komblo's new territory, the story goes, was *wapre* (unoccupied) and rich in marsupials and cassowaries. However, according to accounts, Komblo swiftly entered into exchange relationships with two other neighbouring Wahgi groups, Andpang and Kulaka and, in some versions, the girls and pigs which Komblo are said to have given them are referred to specifically as payment for the land. On the basis of a long interview he had with Aipe, a prominent Jiruka leader, Trompf has argued that Komblo secured the land by celebrating, and then transferring to their neighbours, the institution of the Pig Festival, a major pig-killing rite celebrated in both the Simbu and Wahgi areas (Kondwal and Trompf 1982).

In some respects, the idea that a migrant group like Komblo might have used ritual knowledge in this way is appealing. Such knowledge *is* circulated as a valuable resource among New Guinea Highland peoples. Moreover, specific components of the Pig Festival – sacred flutes, ceremonial wigs (pl. 6) and *geru* boards, and the *bolyim* cult house (pl. 9) built at the climax to the Festival – are recognised among Wahgi groups more generally as diffusing westward from a Simbu origin. However, while some Komblo do agree, if specifically asked, that the original immigrants traded certain components of the Pig Festival, this information was never volunteered to me. A further difficulty with Trompf's thesis in its specific form has to do with the *bolyim* house in particular. In Trompf's account this was among the items originally imported by Komblo as part of the profound religious change he sees their arrival as

Fig. 7 Komblo Kekanem: changing marriage patterns by decade.

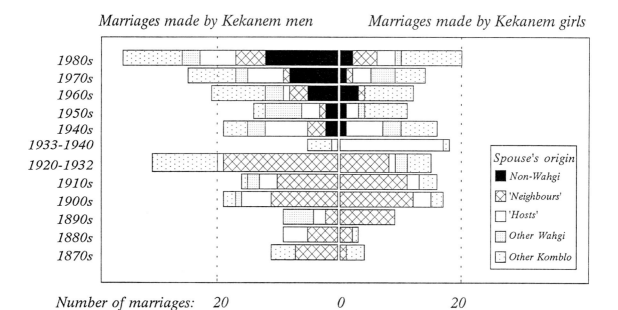

initiating in the area. However, during my own fieldwork in 1979, Komblo ritual leaders re-established contact with their Narku origins precisely in order to purchase the *bolyim* house, as a ritual form which they had left behind on their earlier departure. I would also place Komblo's arrival somewhat earlier than the 1860 estimated by Trompf.

For Komblo, this story of their exodus 'from the stony places downriver' explains how they come to be where they are, provides a mythological grounding for such points as the long-standing alliance with Waka tribe and the unequal amounts of land possessed by particular Komblo clans, and lists the clans themselves. Thereafter, the immigrants are said to have produced sets of sons who in turn became the founders of further subgroups within Komblo. It is not clear how swiftly they ceased to speak a Simbu language but there is, for example, no memory among the oldest people of their grandparental generation ever recalling any language but Wahgi being spoken. Nor was there any maintenance of marriage ties with Narku, which would anyway have been unusual in pre-contact times over the distance which now separated them. Instead, Komblo were most heavily intermarried with their neighbours in the Wahgi: Kumnika, Andpang, Sekaka and Kulaka. This is clear from fig. 7, which is based on the marriages made by Kekanem, one of the main subgroups of Ngunzka.

'Excreting up-river, drinking downstream'

While some New Guinea Highlands peoples say 'we marry the people we fight' (Meggitt 1965:101), the Wahgi more often think of the relationship between intermarried groups as an amicable one. It is recognised, however, that this ideal may not always be met, and there are cultural rules, when intermarried groups do fall out, which forbid men to engage directly in warfare against their 'sources', their mothers' brothers' subclans. Komblo's relationships with their new neighbours had featured such periods of warfare, just as the neighbours – and indeed Komblo clans themselves   also fought each other. Towards the close of the 1920s, however, the fighting between Komblo and their neighbours seems to have escalated. For some years Komblo had been involved in what they call the Mol-Wolo war, a protracted, if intermittent, war with their formidable eastern neighbours, Kumnika. Though Komblo were initially assisted by their own western neighbours Sekaka, by some Kulaka further to the west, as well as by co-resident Sekainnge refugees, by the end of the 1920s they found themselves facing an overwhelming coalition, whose composition Komblo men list today as an indication of the number of opponents it took to expel them as refugees.

It is not totally clear how Komblo came to find themselves so isolated. One factor seems to have been their very success in killing as many Kumnika as they say they did at a famous ambush at the Kumuk stream, a deed which is said to have redoubled Kumnika enmity. Another was the defection of many of their erstwhile Sekaka allies, who split along the pre-existing fissure lines of marriage relations with Komblo. One account, from the senior Sekaka man Paple Kerenga (fig. 8), attributes the defection of half of Sekaka to their anger at a Komblo decision to give two brides elsewhere, rather than to Sekaka. Paple Kerenga recalls his father throwing his bow to the ground in rejection upon hearing of the Sekaka resolution to change sides, for Komblo were among his father's 'source people'. But Sekaka Kolip picked the bow up, declaring '*you* may be born of a Komblo woman (*Komblo amb kusil*) so will not fight them, but *I* am not: let us attack Komblo!'.[6]

Men of Komblo Ngunzka, in particular, see as important in their defeat by this coalition the killing of two of their notable warriors, Ka and Tai. To this day, Ngunzka men remain troubled by these deaths, unsure that all the circumstances surrounding them have been fully revealed. During a period of temporary peace, Ka had been sent a Kumnika Tunjkup girl in marriage, an act which Komblo now recognise as 'tethering her as bait'. When, a few days later, the girl returned to visit her kin, Ka followed her and was killed in a dawn ambush. The news of his death was shouted across the Kar River to Komblo, where Tai refused to be dissuaded from investigating. As Tai crossed the Anye stream *en route*, the cord fastening his bark belt (fig. 9) snapped; Koi, a fellow clansman accompanying Tai, cautioned him that this was a warning from his father's ghost against proceeding. Tai nevertheless forged ahead, out-distancing those with him, but was seized on arrival. He was wear-

Fig. 8 Paple Kerenga is a noted producer of plaited cane armbands (1990).

ing a headdress of horizontally-mounted Lesser bird of paradise plumes, with an upright heron's wing projecting above a cassowary topknot. His companions describe how the last they saw of Tai alive was the heron's wing waving as he was killed, his arms being held away from his body.

Ka and Tai's bodies were brought home by Komblo maternal kin and cross-cousins amongst Sekaka, enraged by their killing. The military pressure against Komblo was now becoming insupportable and they withdrew to Ongmange (fig. 10), the massive buttress which overlooks the Kar Valley. From Ongmange, Komblo engaged in a series of increasingly bitter encounters with their opponents, mutually driving each other to further excesses by mutilating the corpses of the dead, women dying in night-time forays to harvest sweet potato. This fighting was never in fact classified as the most bitter form of Wahgi warfare, known after the red plumes worn for it as 'Raggiana bird of paradise warfare'. The period is nevertheless deeply inscribed on the consciousness of those Komblo who lived through it. Individuals recall the predicament of finding themselves with torn loyalties, ranged against groups containing close kin – though Komblo also say that their opponents described them at this time as heedless of their obligations to maternal kin and affines, as 'fighting with their eyes closed', as 'excreting up-river then drinking downstream'. It is also during this confused and intense period of warfare that

Fig. 9 Incised bark belt (contemporary). 1990 Oc.9.490; H: 11.4 cm.

Fig. 10 Ongmange, the buttress at the head of the Kar Valley; today, coffee shade-trees cover the valley floor (1990).

Komblo and their neighbours suspect many of the hidden betrayals and killings of 'source' people took place – actions whose effects are felt to resonate as death and infertility to the present. As fig. 7 indicates, this period of bitter conflict also inaugurated an almost complete taboo, which was to last for fifty years, on further marriage (and other fraternising) with the neighbouring tribes with whom Komblo had hitherto been most heavily intermarried.[7]

Finally, when all their pigs had been cooked and eaten and men were too weak from hunger to support their heavy shields any longer, Komblo fled Ongmange at night, stowing their valuables in netbags, and dressing young boys (such as my sponsor Kinden) in skirts to disguise their sex in an effort to prevent their being killed should they be intercepted *en route*. As indicated above, many Komblo went initially to relatives in Senglap, to the east. Others, such as Kekanem, a major subgroup of Ngunzka, fled south across the Wahgi River to relatives amongst Kurup-Maiamka: some losing their way, petrified that the whimpering of their children would reveal them, others narrowly avoiding a party of Kumnika enemies returning from a courting party. Looking back from the other side of the valley, they saw their houses had been torched on Ongmange.

1933 – c.1940

When the Leahy-Taylor patrol arrived in April 1933, then, Komblo were refugees, scattered in different parts of the valley. But in contrast with the experience of many of the Papuan societies first contacted by the Hides-O'Malley expedition, who were not to see outsiders again for a decade or more, the arrival of the Leahy-Taylor patrol presaged much swifter consolidation. In July 1933, the Leahys located sufficient gold to begin small-scale mining near Mt. Hagen, other prospectors passed through, and there was a rush by Catholic and Lutheran missionaries who competed to establish bases in Simbu and near Mt. Hagen (Mennis 1982). Hughes (1978:315) notes that by 1938, employees of the Administration, missions and miners near Mt. Hagen totalled between 700 and 800 men; to pay them, vast quantities of shells were airlifted into the Highlands. Pearl shells were first freighted in from Manus, and subsequently from Thursday Island in the Torres Strait in a chartered DC3 aircraft, 'a £1,000 load fetching ten times the price at Mt. Hagen' (*op. cit.*: 313). Thursday Island was also a source for bailer shells (fig. 11), while green snail, cowrie and dog-whelk were imported from various other points on the coast. Such was the appetite for shell in the Highlands that securing sufficient supplies was a periodic problem. White saucers were tried as alternatives for bailer shell forehead ornaments, and the Lutheran mission had imitation egg-cowries made in Birmingham in England.

The importation of shell and other valuables had an immediate effect on local social and economic relations. Those groups near Mt. Hagen, in whose territories Whites had settled, had a considerable advantage over their immediate neighbours in terms of access to shells, steel tools and other goods. Shell and steel, moreover, could now be acquired merely in return for food, whereas in the past they were only to be had in return for equivalently high-value items and in marriage exchanges. The fact that shells were now being imported by air also had implications for the relationship between groups in

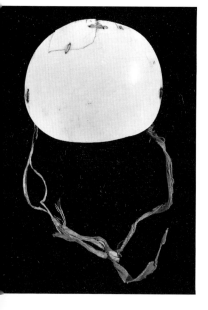

Fig. 11 Forehead ornament of bailer shell, showing local repair; 1990 Oc.9.324; W: 12.6 cm.

the central Highlands and those more towards the periphery, who now no longer controlled the trade routes along which shells had formerly made their way into the centre. A.J. Strathern (1971) has interpreted cargo cults in the 1940s south of Mt. Hagen as an attempt to recapture this lost advantage. Despite the local appetite for shell, inflation also set in almost immediately: 'We have a price war on our hands', Mick Leahy was writing in April 1934, 'they are demanding two gold-lip pearl shells or one gold-lip and a tomahawk, which is impossible – a gold-lip costs 2/6d in Salamaua and 4/6d airfreight, so needs a reasonable sized pig' (cited in Hughes *op. cit.*: 312). Meanwhile, further to the east, the Tuman stone axe mines, where mining was actually in progress on the day the first plane flew over, were abandoned.

While the valley served as a corridor along which the incomers made their way to and from Mt. Hagen and beyond, no mission or administrative stations were established in the mid-Wahgi area itself. Individual Komblo were, however, co-opted. One such was the remarkable Ngunzka Kekanem man, Ond Koi. As Ond Koi (pl. 5) tells the story today, James Taylor instructed one of his policemen to find a boy to be turned into an interpreter. Police at that time were buying food in return for cowrie shells and salt; in trying to trade, Ond Koi, who was then in his mid-teens and living with Kurup-Maiamka (map 2) along with other Kekanem refugees, was caught and handcuffed to a policeman. His mother cried, he says, but Taylor gave her cowrie shells, some red cloth, salt, a mirror, a knife and an axe, and told her that he was taking her son to Kainantu in the far east of the Highlands, to train him as an interpreter. There Ond Koi stayed for a year or two, he says, learning the lingua franca, Pidgin English, before being made interpreter to the patrol officer in charge at Kundiawa in today's Simbu Province.

Komblo meanwhile continued to suffer the drawbacks attendant on refugee status, forced to surrender their adolescent daughters as wives to their hosts

in return for tumbledown houses,
in return for overgrown sweet potato gardens.

Equally, as 'refugees, without pigs or wealth', few Komblo men could marry. Both these points are reflected in fig. 7 which shows that of those few Kekanem men who *did* marry over the period of their refugeeship almost all took other Komblo girls as wives, while virtually all Kekanem girls who married went to 'host' men. Men's difficulty in marrying may also have precipitated intermarriage between the two Komblo subgroups of Jiruka and Kulka, which had hitherto been considered too closely related to do so. The fact that the first marriage, between Jiruka Aipe and the Kulka girl Ningn, produced a son was taken as a sign that the step had the approval of ancestral ghosts.

Nor, despite their refugee status, did Komblo feel safe from those who had ousted them. Wahgi suspect that men unable or unwilling to kill their enemies directly may bribe intermediaries to do so, giving them shell wealth, with perhaps a thread from a skirt attached as a sign that a bride would also be bestowed once the killing was achieved. A number of Komblo deaths during this period are attributed to the '*engk* spear', as this form of contract killing, whether direct or through poison, is known. Again, the consequences of these covert actions reverberate still. To this day, deaths and infertility among brides may be traced to the fact that they have unknowingly married amongst groups

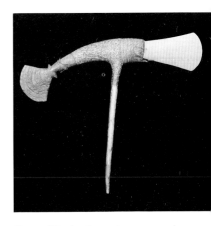

Fig. 12 'The battle-axe is a work of art' (Mount Hagen Patrol Report). 1936.7–20.265; L: 54 cm.

who had previously contracted to slay the bride's own kin; or reciprocally, whom the bride's kin had previously pledged to kill.

Fears of the '*engk* spear' and inevitable quarrels with their hosts thus kept the Komblo refugees on the move. Some of those resident with Senglap moved further east to live with Waka, celebrated for the help they gave the original Komblo immigrants in crossing the flooded Ga River. Others moved south to live with Peripka, and then back again after Kulka Kolnga had cuckolded one of his Peripka hosts – the Komblo contingent slipping away with the girls they had promised Peripka in marriage, cutting the vine bridge over the Wahgi River behind them.

In this situation Komblo attempted to use the new White presence in the area, and their links to it through the interpreter Ond Koi, to secure their return to their territory on the Kar River. As Gordon and Meggitt (1985:166-7) have described, interpreters occupied influential 'gate-keeping' positions, able to determine access to patrol officers, and Ond Koi's mediation is recognised by other Komblo as eventually securing a favourable hearing for a number of Komblo representatives. Taylor detailed a squad of police to assemble and oversee the return of the refugees. This was duly achieved, the returning Komblo being welcomed back by wailing affines and maternal kin from amongst their neighbours.

Relatives amongst Waplka, the Sekaka group least involved in Komblo's expulsion, provided the returnees with food and houses on their Ongmange citadel. Some Komblo men, however, were so affected by returning to their land that, it is said, they slept directly on the ground, outside without fires. The police who escorted them back (whose names, such as Pike, Nake and Aipanga, have since been included within Komblo's stock of names) also engaged in a number of displays of force designed to deter Komblo's neighbours from further attacks: making them bite stones, in some accounts also raping women and shooting a pig-rustler *en route*. At this time, too, various of Komblo's maternal and affinal kin amongst their neighbours are also said secretly to have presented Komblo with house-posts and plant cuttings. In so doing, the donors were deliberately sabotaging their own clansmen's capacity ever again to expel Komblo as refugees, for the recipients of such gifts are believed to derive overwhelming strength from holding these tokens of earlier goodwill.

'*Offspring of mission and Administration*'

While the documents which might have dated the restoration of Komblo to their territory appear not to have survived, their return must have taken place around 1940, for Komblo were back at the Kar River by the beginning of the Pacific War. Though the Japanese ground forces which invaded New Guinea in 1942 never reached the Highlands proper, Komblo recall their fear of the formations of planes they saw overhead – an alarm, they say, which was shared by a party of Australian soldiers who camped in Komblo territory for a week and were fed by them. These Australians were apparently retreating from Japanese forces further to the north, and are recalled in part for being led by a short, immensely muscular man whose name, remembered as 'Tonkye', was incorporated into a Komblo courting song of the time. Some

Komblo were involved in the fighting: Kekanem Nin was injured by a bomb dropped near Mt. Hagen, which became a significant centre during the war, being visited by celebrities such as John Wayne. Ond Koi, who had been made a policeman, also served during the war, as did Kekanem Bamne.

Such obvious repercussions of the Pacific War were, however, of less lasting significance to many Komblo than was one effect which was interpreted in indigenous terms. Burton (1983) has analysed the dysentery epidemic which the war brought to the Highlands between 1943-5, and the subsequent mortality. A spate of deaths, almost certainly from dysentery, was attributed by the Komblo subgroup affected to the activities of poisoners within the clan and ensuing ghostly retribution from the victims. In the case in question, the suspected poisoners (said to have been aggrieved with their clan brothers over the disposal of a girl in marriage) are thought to have used the funeral feast of the first of their victims to insert poison into the food of the next. The affected subgroup recall how people died one after the other, their intestines 'bursting', ending with the death of one of the poisoners.

Here there was an awful coincidence between the Wahgi preoccupation with betrayal, the rites they perform at death and the epidemiology of dysentery. Each of the successive funeral feasts, involving as they do the communal sharing of food, would have been an effective vector for the transmission of the dysentery, while the ensuing deaths seemed to confirm that poisoners were indeed at work within. This local interpretation must have been strengthened by the fact that, in the case of the deaths of important men or of people who died unexpectedly, funeral feasts were explicitly divinatory. Grime from the corpse's nose was wiped onto a bamboo knife which was then used to cut up the funeral pigs, whose meat would, it was thought, shortly choke the guilty party. It is difficult to overestimate the impact of such a spate of deaths in a society whose explanations of causality involve both internal betrayals and ghostly retribution, while also allowing considerable uncertainty and the possibility of politically-motivated accusations. Great intellectual energy is deployed over the years in attempting to make sense of such deaths as a linked series, and in assessing further deaths, infertility or poor appearance as evidence for one theory or another. The instituting of separating taboos, shifts in residence away from suspected traitors and, in the past, their precipitate execution, were frequent results.

The epidemic eventually ran its course, its end hastened by treatment with the new drug sulphaguanidine. The post-war period saw a rapid White reconsolidation, once restrictions on White residence were lifted in 1947 (Luzbetak 1958:55). In 1948, the millionaire Australian refrigerator manufacturer Hallstrom established his Livestock and Fauna Trust at Nondugl in the northeast section of the Wahgi. The subdistrict headquarters was set up at Minj in 1952, and systematic patrolling was instituted, aimed at producing detailed demographic information[8] and ending inter-group fighting. Corrigan, the Assistant District Officer at Minj, noted in his South Wahgi patrol report of 1952-3 that he did 'not think that any embers of martial ardour continue to glow' in the area. The names of these early Whites, 'Masta Korkan', 'Masta Noman', 'Masta Pulaka' have a prominent place in the imagination of the young Komblo men and other Wahgi who now began to seek employment with them.

Initially, such work was paid for directly in axes and in shells, bringing to a close the pre-contact trading patterns in which almost all shells had 'originated up-river and moved in a down-river direction'.[9] And whereas in the past Wahgi had received shells ready worked into ornaments, they now had to learn to cut and polish them themselves. Sillitoe (1988:382) has described for another Highlands people, the Wola, the gamble represented by unworked pearl shells: until it is cut and polished a shell's final colour, a matter of considerable concern, is not apparent. The Wahgi, like the Wola, prefer pearl shells to have as deep a red-gold lustre as possible. These shells, 'flickering with red fire', are spoken of as reserved for such special tasks as bribing assassins and for decoration, in contrast to paler and larger pearl shells thought more appropriate for giving in bridewealth. Sometimes a pig would be sacrificed before commencing work on cutting a pearl shell. The increasing availability of the more highly prized pearl and bailer shells was probably also a factor in changes in decoration styles around this time. The fashion for mounting cowrie shells on long bands of barkcloth and wearing them like crossed bandoleers was discarded, as were most of the 'bonnets' of cowrie or dog whelk shells which can be seen in Leahy's pictures; nose disks also ceased to be made from the cheaper alternatives of wood or stone, and were manufactured only from conus shell.

From the late 1940s, the Australian Administration began to introduce a money economy in the Wahgi. Today older Komblo recall their interest in currency and their reservations about it. Watermarks and designs were thought by some to be representations of money's ancestral owners who might return to claim it; consequently, notes were passed on very hurriedly. As they ceased to be paid directly in shell, Wahgi began to use money to buy shells from the trade-stores. Whether shell was acquired in direct payment, or by way of cash, it is clear that the highly bedecked appearance of Wahgi in photographs from this period was substantially a colonial artefact (see pl. 4). It was the Australian Administration which had imported most of the shell, just as it imposed the peace in which ceremonial payments of shell could flourish.

Young Komblo men also began to earn wealth further afield, working on the Highlands Labour Scheme, and on the patrols which from the late 1940s began to establish administrative centres and aerodromes in the hitherto neglected Southern Highlands and Enga Provinces. These patrols – 'bush work' – and the patrol officers who led them, are remembered in a dirge whose slow pace reflects, perhaps, their arduousness:

> *Masta Lea-o, wok bus-o*
> *Oi mai-o, pwi-o e*
> *Masta Lea-o, wok bus-o*
> *Oi mai-o, pwi-o e!*

Such expeditions may also be recalled as the origin of long-term marriage links with non-Wahgi groups. Komblo Kekanem, for example, developed such a relationship with the people of Arumanda (map 1), one small area of what was to become Enga Province. Since the late 1940s, a dozen girls have come in marriage to Kekanem, or to close relatives of Kekanem, from this same area – the earlier ones acting as the 'path' along which later brides have come (fig. 13). Such marriages initiate the trend, clearly shown in fig. 7, whereby

Plate 1 View south across the Wahgi Valley from Komblo territory. The track along the 'well defined grass covered ridge' traversed by the Leahy-Taylor patrol in 1933 is clearly visible. (1979)

Plate 2 1950s bridewealth banner. During the 1950s, bridewealth was mainly paid in the burgeoning shell wealth and in red Raggiana bird of paradise plumes, with only a few of the black Stephanie plumes which later became important. *Photograph by kind permission of Stan Christian.*

Plate 3 1980 bridewealth banner. The cash which was given in bridewealth during the 1970s and into the 1980s was presented in the same way as shells had been previously; by this point black Stephanie and Sicklebill plumes had displaced red Raggiana feathers. (1980)

Plate 5 During the 1970s, cartons of beer were incorporated into local inter-clan exchanges; here Kekanem Ond Koi (seated left of cartons) receives a return gift of beer and food from his Omngar 'source people'. (1980)

Plate 4 Into the 1980s, the occasional elderly man continued to wear the elaborate shell ornaments more characteristic of earlier decades. (1980)

Plate 6 Pig Festival dances are the peak of Wahgi visual performance; here wig-wearers head a phalanx of dancers from Komblo's Kulka clan. (1979)

Plate 7 James Bosu at the height of the Sekaka Pig Festival. The late 1970s boom in coffee prices was reflected in increased Wahgi imports of the costly black plumes and also of beer. (1979)

Plate 8 Eating pork fat on platforms at the climax to the Komblo Pig Festival; here Are and Pilei (wearing red and blue *geru* board) share a side of pork. (1980)

Komblo men have increasingly married girls from beyond the Wahgi area: in particular, girls from areas which are either less developed or less wealthy, such as Enga, the Southern Highlands, and Simbu. Those few Komblo girls who have married non-Wahgi men, in contrast, have tended to marry relatively wealthy individuals, in waged employment. This marks the start of the formation of an asymmetric relationship between the Wahgi and these other areas, a relationship whose inequality was soon to be compounded by the development of coffee as a cash crop in the Wahgi.

Fig. 13 Kema (left), an inmarried wife from Enga, chats to Ner, another Kekanem wife (1990).

There was also a variety of consequences for social relationships within the Wahgi. With young men able to earn shell wealth directly from Whites, they no longer needed to work for older men in return for the loan of shell ornaments for courting purposes. Again, girls who resented the husbands chosen for them found that they could invoke patrol officers to defend *laik bilong meri*: women's wishes. Girls could no longer be forced so overtly into sister-exchange and other marriage arrangements they disliked – though their parents found themselves still expected to control the marriage destinations of their daughters in terms of the calculus of clan advantage and indebtedness. A Patrol Officer had noted optimistically in 1959 that 'The traditional system of arranging daughters' marriages has been stopped by the administration' (Patrol Report No. 1, 1959/60). In fact, parents continued to exert great moral pressure, and on occasion considerable physical violence, to dissuade daughters from particular marriages, or to compel them into others. Nevertheless an overall reduction in compulsion perhaps explains the greater rapidity with which the first instalment of bridewealth began to be paid. In the past, people say, this first instalment was not made over until a bride had proved herself by wearing down her fingernails working in the sweet potato gardens.

A girl's kin may require swifter evidence of the capacity to pay bridewealth from a husband whom she has herself chosen.

It was around this time – the mid-1950s – that in bitter circumstances the large Komblo clan of Ngunzka split into the separate, and eventually inter-marrying, clans of Kekanem and Anzkanem. In fact, in a spectacular example of blaming the victim, Ngunzka men sometimes hold one of the newly in-married Enga girls to be responsible for this shattering of their unity as a single exogamous group who together:

> ate the things that are for eating,
> gave the things that are for giving

(i.e. who shared bridewealth for out-marrying sisters and purchased wives as a single clan). The Engan girl in question, Kesamb, had married a man from the Ngunzka clan-section of Kekanem. She was raped, or perhaps violently propositioned, by a man from the opposite clan-section, Anzkanem. This led to intra-clan fighting, a not uncommon occurrence but one in which weapons were traditionally restricted to long sticks and parry shields, rather than axes, spears and the panoply of full warfare adornment. However, rumours that an injured Anzkanem man was near to death lent the fighting a new intensity, and Simbil, a Kekanem man, was fatally clubbed. Anzkanem now fled, taking refuge for a while with relatives amongst their fellow tribespeople of Jiruka and Kulka clans, and Kekanem and Anzkanem became taboo to each other. They remained so for the next eleven years, at which point Anzkanem presented a bride to Kekanem as compensation for Simbil's death and, amid the anguish which attends the notion of a hitherto solidary group splitting, Kekanem and Anzkanem became separate clans.

Subsequently, and initially only very cautiously, further brides have been exchanged between the two groups. However, the affair resonates to this day. The physical appearance of such brides (the condition of their 'skin'), and whether or not they have children, continues to be used as evidence in at least three ongoing arguments: whether the formal separation of Kekanem and Anzkanem has ancestral approval; which of the Anzkanem subclans Simbil's killer truly came from (in the mêlée there was some doubt as to the precise identity of his killers[10]); and whether internal problems among Kekanem subclans have been resolved, bearing in mind that Simbil's subclan is owed compensation by Kesamb's husband's subclan, since it was her rape that led to his death.[11]

This continued divinatory use of appearance and fertility raises the issue of the impact of Christianity on the Wahgi. By the mid-1950s missions had been established at various points in the area. Catholics were installed at Nondugl, and around Banz no less than three missions were represented: Catholics, Lutherans and a small contingent of Seventh Day Adventists. The SDA were the forerunners of a rush of fundamentalist missions; by 1990, these included the Nazarenes, the Swiss Mission (later known as the Evangelical Brotherhood Church), Jehovah's Witnesses and the Apostolic Church. Over time, the various missions have become dominant in different parts of the Wahgi. Most Komblo, for example, are Catholics, though they also include some Lutherans and an increasing number of adherents to fundamentalist churches. Nazarenes are particularly strong around Kudjip, where the mission also runs an excellent hospital, and the Evangelical Brotherhood Church is influential in the Minj area.

This mission presence has had a notable impact on the form of Wahgi religion and on Wahgi culture more generally. Traditional day-to-day Wahgi religious practices revolved around attempts to secure the support of ancestral ghosts, and to deflect their wrath, through divination and subsequent pig sacrifices. Missions of all stripes have campaigned against such pig sacrifices, which are now seldom performed in an overt way. However, the fact that the different missions also vary in their approach to the project of conversion gives a different look to Wahgi culture in the various parts of the valley. The Catholic Mission, for example, supports a more gradualist approach. Encouragement is given to particular aspects of local culture, such as the wearing of traditional adornment by schoolchildren once a week. In Catholic areas, the climactic event of Wahgi religious life, the Pig Festival, has also continued to be performed, though often with Christian crosses erected alongside the *bolyim* house and *mond* post (pl. 9). The more fundamentalist missions, in contrast, emphasise conversion as a radical break, in which much of local culture is identified as unambiguously bad. An Evangelical Brotherhood Church flip chart, for example, depicts a bird of paradise, a cassowary and a pig cohabiting a black, unredeemed heart along with the devil, a snake etc. Over the succeeding pages of the chart, these manifestations of heathenism are put to flight by rays, emanating from the Bible, which also lighten the black heart.

At the same time, it would be wrong to think of Wahgi as no more than the passive recipients of 'conversion'. As Reay (1971:179) has noted, South Wall Wahgi accepted mission proposals to exorcise their war-magic houses in 1965 partly 'because it offered a safe means of removing taboos on sharing food . . . which had become extremely inconvenient in the circumstances of modern life. The simple ignoring of these taboos would not suffice, since flouting them was to invite death'. Here missions served as a device through which Wahgi could adapt local culture to contemporary circumstances[12] – rather as Hawaiian chiefs sometimes disposed of ritually dangerous feather cloaks by giving them to Europeans (Kaeppler 1992:462). Equally, there is evidence to suggest that the decision by a number of Komblo individuals and subgroups to affiliate to missions different from those of their fellow clanspeople reflected pre-existing enmities and splits; their differential affiliation, in other words, was partly a medium through which to pursue local political issues.

It would be equally wrong to think of Christianity, in whichever form, merely as replacing a concern with ghosts. Ghosts continue to be thought of as a potent force behind much of what goes on in social life, even though many of the overt practices intended to influence them have vanished. From one point of view, God has been slotted in at the top of the cosmology, as a figure who 'looks after' ancestral ghosts, who are nevertheless thought on occasion to 'slip away' to injure kinsfolk who have displeased them. From another perspective, as A.J. Strathern (1984:33) has pointed out for the Wiru, mission influence in a sense positively requires the continuing existence of indigenous spirit categories – as antagonists against which a Christian must strive. Ancestral ghosts 'remain as real as ever, but are now designated as wholly bad, hostile and dangerous, whereas God is good, loving and beneficent'. Thus Wahgi now often refer to ghosts as *tantan* ('Satan'). In short, the process of religious change is less a displacement of old forms by new than an incorporative process, one in which Wahgi are active agents rather than purely passive vessels for Christian doctrine. Certainly, Komblo recall the Seventh Day Adventist ban on the consumption of pork as more than they were prepared to stomach: they say they burned down the base the mission established on local ground.

Coffee

Local missions also served as a further source of employment for the Wahgi. Then, in the mid-1950s, expatriates established coffee plantations on the flat, largely unoccupied valley floor. With its high value-to-weight ratio, coffee was a particularly appropriate export crop for what in global terms was still a relatively remote area. Highlands coffee is also of high quality, and manufacturers often selectively add it to their instant coffees to enhance the taste. For a while, such plantation work was a further source of local employment, but within a year or two Wahgi also began to grow coffee on their own account. Among Komblo, it was Ond Koi, the former interpreter and policeman, who is credited with being the first to plant seedlings, brought home with him from Goroka. Fellow clansmen recall both the derision with which senior men greeted Ond Koi's planting of this apparently useless crop and Ond Koi's response: that in time those who now mocked him would be sweeping up the leavings from his activities. In fact, however, other Komblo swiftly stole seedlings from coffee plantations to establish their own stands of trees, pre-empting what appears to have been a somewhat ambivalent government attitude towards local 'village' coffee-growing.

Once the trees were bearing fruit, 'village' coffee production rose sharply: in 1963/4 output was 350 tons, the following year it was 550 tons (Minj Patrol Report No. 8 for 1965/6). By 1967/8, despite a slump in coffee prices to half their previous level, the value of local production was over $A500,000. Wage-labour – whether on expatriate-owned plantations or elsewhere – came to be increasingly unattractive to Wahgi as a means of earning cash, by comparison with tending their own coffee (fig. 14). Wahgi reluctance to work on plantations, except as a short-term expedient to meet the introduced head tax, is a *leit-motif* in patrol reports during the 1960s. As one report noted somewhat plaintively, expatriate planters tended to forget that 'the bulk of these people are completely independent and their present immediate needs are obtainable with the minimum of effort'.[13]

Increasingly, therefore, plantations in the Wahgi came to be worked by labour migrants from other parts of the Highlands, in particular from Simbu, from the Jimi Valley to the north, from Enga and later from the Southern Highlands: areas which were over-populated, less-developed or climatically unsuited to growing coffee. Some Wahgi men themselves began to employ such labour migrants, sometimes also inviting in their families, in part to increase clan strength. This was a process which alarmed Administration officials, concerned that it would lead to land shortage in the Wahgi itself. Meanwhile, the net inflow of women from these less-advantaged areas, so clear from the Komblo data, continued elsewhere in the Wahgi. Minj Patrol Report

Fig. 14 Kilyen (left) and Maime weigh and bag dried coffee beans (1990).

No.1 for 1966/7, for example, noted that while fourteen girls from the Minj area (map 2) had married into Simbu, no less than sixty Simbu brides had married into Minj, many being followed by their relatives.

Wahgi deployed this coffee income in a variety of ways. From this period dates the replacement of much of their material culture by imported equivalents. Luzbetak (1958:58-9), writing towards the end of the 1950s, remarked on the plates, cups, bowls, boxes, blankets and other clothing which were now to be found in Wahgi houses – particularly in those houses closer to government stations, plantations and missions, which had greater access to money. Correspondingly, items like wooden pandanus processing bowls, oil funnels (fig. 15) and barkcloth beaters (like stone axes earlier) ceased to

Fig. 15 Oil funnel. Pork fat is placed in the body of the funnel, hot stones added, and the resulting oil poured off into a gourd container. 1990 Oc.9.567; L: 54 cm.

Fig. 16 Wicker container for drying pandanus nuts; soot-encrusted from storage in house-roof. 1990 Oc.9.562; L: 128 cm.

be made in such areas – though other artefacts, such as the long wicker cages in which pandanus nuts are dried, and for which durable imported substitutes were not available, continued to be produced (fig. 16).

Coffee income was also spent on the import of huge numbers of bird of paradise plumes of varieties uncommon in the Wahgi. The later 1950s and 1960s saw the replacement, as the dominant feathers used in headdresses and bridewealth payments, of the locally-available red Raggiana plumes by the long black Stephanie and Sicklebill plumes commoner in Central, Morobe and Enga Provinces (fig. 17). The relative rarity of these plumes in the Wahgi may have been one reason for their adoption: their possession would have marked out those who controlled the new valuable of money, and their fragility would have helped maintain their worth (Heaney 1982, O'Hanlon 1989). Money was also included in increasing amounts in bridewealth and other inter-group payments; by the end of the 1960s it had almost entirely displaced pearl shells in this role. Some pearl shells have been retained as items of adornment. Others were off-loaded in exchange with peripheral areas (which still valued them) such as the Jimi Valley, where the trading system came to be structured round supplying Stephanie and Sicklebill plumes to the Wahgi (Healey 1990). Bridewealth and other inter-group payments within the Wahgi began rapidly to inflate, a topic which preoccupied Patrol Reports during the 1960s.

As with missionisation, however, it is easy to be misled by changes in external form into overlooking continuities. As Thomas (1991:108) has argued much more broadly, the uses to which things imported into the Pacific may be put are not 'inscribed in them by their metropolitan producers'. In some ways, Wahgi treated money as they did the shells it replaced. Like shells, money may be used to decorate the person and, until the 1980s, it was arrayed in the same way that shells were on the banners on which bridewealth is displayed for presentation (pls. 2, 3 and 16). In Healey's (1990:200-1) terms, money was incorporated not simply as a currency, a general measure of the value of all things, but as itself a category of valuable – like shells, pigs or plumes. As Healey (*loc. cit.*) has also argued, the use of money in exchanges has led anthropologists to assume that it functions as currency revealing a price. This is not necessarily so: for example throughout the last thirteen years, a pair of armbands has conventionally been exchanged in the Wahgi for K4, although the prices of items sold over the counter in shops have increased considerably during this period.

This may be why Wahgi, and other Highlanders who also incorporated money into their exchange systems as a valuable, appear not to have developed any concept of 'bitter money'. A number of Latin American and African

Fig. 17 A bride is decorated in Princess Stephanie bird of paradise plumes; Golomb (right) inserts the plumes in Kos's headdress (1990).

societies make a distinction between 'good' money, and money that is 'bitter' or 'sterile' and which has to be ritually purified or baptised before it can be put to productive use (Shipton 1989). The distinction between the two kinds of money appears to be made in circumstances of strain produced by growing involvement in a cash economy, with the consequent erosion of local solidarities. While this is undoubtedly happening in certain respects in the Wahgi, the fact that money was incorporated as a valuable of the order of pigs, plumes and shells, may have suppressed the development of the notion of a morally perilous, 'bitter' kind of money. In fact, in drawing money into the exchange system, senior men were assimilating it to the pre-existing category of 'valuable', which they – as opposed to women or young men – traditionally controlled (A.J. Strathern 1979a).

Money was also increasingly spent on a range of introduced foods, particularly rice and tinned fish. These were sold retail through the small trade-stores which Wahgi men, and the occasional woman, began to establish. By the mid-1960s, there were over a hundred such stores in the subdistrict.[14] In time, a considerable range of other goods came to be sold through these stores: tobacco, soft drinks, tea, sugar, salt, crackers, dripping, items for body adornment, and acrylic yarns for making netbags. Trade-stores tend to be constructed as separate buildings rather than being run from the owner's house. This is probably partly an attempt to establish them as *bisnis*, operating outside the ethic of sharing which should otherwise characterise community life. Certainly, a high proportion of trade-stores have the Pidgin words '*No ken askim long dinau*' (Don't ask for credit) inscribed on the door. Made from corrugated iron (noisier for robbers to break into), trade-stores appear as raw intrusions of commercial morality into a pastoral landscape. In certain respects they are; at the same time, few trade-stores are run on strictly commercial lines, and moreover they also become repositories for such esoteric items as men's love magic which, if kept in ordinary houses, is thought to be injurious to the health of wives and children.

By the mid-1960s, coffee income was also being pooled by clanspeople to purchase vehicles. Estimating that nine had been acquired by South Wall clans alone, a Patrol Officer admitted that 'Clans are buying vehicles both new and second hand so fast that it is difficult to determine just how many there now is [*sic*] . . . they find ample employment with administration contracts and contracts from the twenty-five plantations, not to mention the employment of transporting pigs and brideprices for interclan social exchanges'.[15] He reckoned that such vehicles earned £1,000 per annum, although four years later another Patrol Officer stated that owners had to get the purchase price back within the year if they were not to suffer a loss, so continuously were the vehicles driven on rough roads.[16] Gradually, trucks gave way to buses as the means of transport around the developing road network, the main roads of which were also sealed. By the late 1980s mini-buses, now ornamented by sign painters with such legends as 'Heartbreak Express' or 'Six to Six' (a term for a 6pm to 6am party) were the most popular acquisitions (pl. 12). Scores of such vehicles can be seen in Mt. Hagen town, from which barkers urgently call out their destinations ('Kudjip-Banz! Kudjip-Banz!'), while the drivers

Fig. 18 During the 1980s, buses supplanted trucks as the means to travel the expanding Highlands road network (1990).

themselves edge their vehicles forward in an effort to persuade potential passengers of the imminence of departure (fig. 18).

Such vehicles, known as 'PMV's (Public Motor Vehicles) are a major agency through which the Wahgi area is increasingly integrated with much of the rest of the country. They both facilitate and promote the extended range of marriages seen in microcosm in fig. 7 – the recent film *Tinpis Run* captures something of the sense of flux and mobility engendered by PMVs. At the same time, vehicles (like money) are also re-contextualised in certain respects as distinctively Wahgi. Vehicles are, for example, thought of as an agency through which ghosts may register their attitude towards their living kinsfolk: purchasers of cars may sacrifice pigs or chickens in an endeavour to prevent their vehicles from crashing. Equally, vehicles are regarded as a mechanism through which unresolved anger may manifest itself: I recall one Wahgi friend, who had been insulted by his son, refusing to travel home in the same car with him, lest it crash.

A further introduced item purchased with coffee income is alcohol, which was unknown in Papua New Guinea until introduced by Whites. Papua New Guineans were, in fact, legally debarred from drinking until 1962. By the end of that decade, a Patrol Officer in the Wahgi was recording that 'Consumption of alcohol . . . has been strongly embraced by the majority of males'.[17] Perhaps because Papua New Guineans have to some degree inherited Australian drinking patterns (Marshall 1982:6), beer is by far the most popular form in which to drink alcohol. The preferred brands are overwhelmingly 'SP' and 'San Mig': 'South Pacific' and 'San Miguel' (the former company absorbed the latter in 1983). Initially, beer was purchased mainly in hotel bars in centres like Minj. However, since the devolution of liquor licensing powers to the provincial governments, set up in the late 1970s, many licences to operate local taverns have been issued – partly in an effort to control drinking by integrating it into the community, partly because liquor licensing fees and the retail sales tax on liquor are a major revenue source for provincial governments.

Since the early 1960s, consumption of alcohol has risen many times over and, Marshall (1982:10) suggests, has come to symbolise modernity, to stand for 'all the new consumer goods that can be bought with cash'. But as Marshall has also shown, it is local circumstances, not any inherent nature of the substance, which determines the pattern of alcohol consumption. First, both in the Wahgi and elsewhere in Papua New Guinea, drinking tends to be a group phenomenon: few people drink on their own. Since Wahgi organise themselves in clans and subclans, it is not surprising that drinking groups often reflect these organisational principles in one way or another, and questions of clan politics and prestige readily surface during drinking. Secondly, like other Papua New Guineans, Wahgi tend to drink not their own beer, but beer that they have been given: occasionally in formal inter-group exchanges (pl. 5) but more often in the complex reciprocal gifts made between individuals and groups in bars and taverns.

Warry (1982:93) has described a more specific way in which beer drinking has been incorporated into neighbouring Chuave society – as a substitute for the ritual display and consumption of pork. The Wahgi case, too, hints at parallels between beer and pork, more particularly between beer and pork fat. As I have described elsewhere (O'Hanlon 1989:120), Wahgi think of pork fat as promoting growth; in a sense, fat symbolises the growth and fertility sought during the Pig Festival, as well as the ancestral favour on which these qualities are felt to depend. As such, fat is linked to the two ritual structures – the *bolyim* house and *mond* post – erected at the end of the Pig Festival, both of which are also impregnated and topped with pork fat. And at the climax to a Pig Festival, members of the performing clan, along with favoured guests, climb onto specially erected platforms surrounding the ceremonial ground and onto the *bolyim* house at its centre, there to consume great quantities of pork fat (pl. 8). What is suggestive is the way in which Wahgi today emphasise that beer is a necessary accompaniment, to help the pork fat go down. It is also interesting that beer bottles were thought appropriate decoration for the *bolyim* house by two of the three Komblo clans which erected them at their 1980 Pig Festival.

However, beer has also been implicated in a range of negative developments, both in the Wahgi and elsewhere in Papua New Guinea. While gifts of beer are from one point of view a form of investment in social life, they take cash away from other enterprises. Furthermore, alcohol consumption is very largely a male practice, while women are sometimes the victims of drunken male violence. Inebriated drivers and pedestrians cause car accidents, with drinking sometimes also being recalled in mourning songs. Gilma's widow, for example, recalled the sound of her husband's boisterous homecomings when she sang at his death:

> *Binz mene wo, wi geu neua*
> *Mambel mene wo, wi geu neua*
> *Gilma ya Gilma*
> *Bia wi toi, na pilye monua*

> Let me hear your call as you descend to cross Binz River
> Let me hear your call as you come down over Mambel River[18]
> Gilma oh Gilma
> I long to hear your beery call

Alcohol is also implicated in deaths in brawling; it was in attempting to separate inebriated clansmen that the prominent Komblo Jiruka leader, Aipe, was killed in 1976 (Kondwal and Trompf 1982). While this event did not lead to the permanent splitting of Jiruka, as Simbil's death a generation earlier had done for Ngunzka, its effects resonated within Jiruka, and within Komblo more generally, in a similar way.

The money that flowed from coffee was also saved and invested in other businesses. My own Komblo sponsor, Kinden, for example, was influential in establishing and popularising (both in the Wahgi and beyond) a Savings and Loans society set up with Australian assistance in the mid-1970s. Kinden's own marriage to Ner, a Sekaka woman (albeit from Waplka, the section of Sekaka least involved in expelling Komblo as refugees), gave him a readier entrée than many Komblo had to the coalition of their former enemies. Yimbal, Kauwiye and Kaunga, three able sons of the dead Komblo Jiruka leader Aipe, set up a chain of trade-stores across the Wahgi, using (some say) the compensation payments received for their father's death to establish the business. As their trade-store business expanded, and in partnership with their sister's husband Kekanem Tai (named after his father's brother, one of the two warriors whose slaying preceded Komblo's refugeeship), they established a transport company, and purchased stock wholesale, directly from abroad.

All these processes, both of consumption and investment, were greatly boosted by the dramatic rise in coffee prices which took place in 1975-6 (pl. 7), following severe frost damage to the Brazilian crop. Wahgi sometimes remember this period as one during which even children had K20 (c. £14) notes in their pockets. Government legislation in the mid-1970s also smoothed the path for traditional groups to set themselves up as legal entities. Plantations previously owned by expatriates were bought up by the Wahgi Council, and by consortia of local businessmen who financed the purchases in part through sales of shares among clans in the area.

However, some drawbacks of the increasing dependence on coffee income have also manifested themselves. The price paid for coffee on the world market, over which Wahgi producers have no control, has fluctuated considerably over the last thirty years. Although the Wahgi subsistence base remains intact to date and no one lacks for food or housing, swings in coffee prices affect Wahgi access to the cash now necessary for clothing, school fees and hospital treatment, as well as for social expenditure on bridewealth and other inter-group payments. Coffee rust, a disease which began to spread through the Highlands in the mid-1980s, looked at one point as if it might imperil the

Fig. 19 Thomas Tal, home from Port Moresby, has his picture taken by a local photographer at the centre of the bridal party of his clan sister, Wulamb (in black plumes) (1990).

Fig. 20 Contemporary house interior showing *inter alia* bow and arrows (against wall), and extensive use of flattened cardboard boxes (1990).

coffee of those unable to afford expensive chemical deterrents. In the event, it was the intensively cropped, unshaded, plantation coffee which proved to be more susceptible than 'village' coffee. However, the episode did highlight the potential vulnerability of depending so heavily on a single crop. Coffee trees also take up land previously devoted to sweet potato gardens, which have in turn displaced pig pastures. Uneven access of clans to good coffee-growing land also promotes inequality within the Wahgi, as well as between the Wahgi and less fortunately placed peoples. At the same time, while these latent problems are likely to emerge more sharply if the population continues to increase at its present rate, they are difficulties which the inhabitants of those areas less suited to coffee-growing clearly wish they had.

The Pig Festival

During the latter part of the 1970s the clans of both Komblo and – over the other side of the Kar River – Sekaka, were engaged in Pig Festivals. A Pig Festival is, in effect, a massive fertility ceremony, mounted every twenty years or so, lasting years, and designed to secure the future well-being of the performing clan, to reinforce their friendships and to deter their enemies. These Pig Festivals were the second such ceremonies performed in living memory by Komblo and Sekaka clans – the previous ones had climaxed in about 1953. The Festivals which might have been expected a generation before that, in the 1920s, had never taken place, a casualty of the warfare which led to Komblo's expulsion as refugees. In this respect, then, performance of these great ceremonies initially became more regular following contact with the West – in the same way that contact also boosted the number of shells and other elements of the decorative repertoire worn for Festival dancing.

The early stages of a Pig Festival involve a series of rites designed to promote pig growth, and to acquire the decorations (particularly the costly bird of paradise plumes) which a clan needs for the years of dancing involved. Some of these items of adornment are purchased, but many others are acquired from kin in other groups in exchange for pork from the clan's pigs, which will be killed at the end of the Festival. During much of the final year of the Festival, clansmen (and the occasional unmarried girl) decorate and dance on their ceremonial ground two or three times a week. The images from which the swelling dance songs are composed are conventional, drawn from those heard at other Festivals, or even at funerals. This limited stock of metaphors is re-deployed to comment allusively on the current state of political relations. For example, Gilma's widow's lament (recorded on p.42) was said to have been the source for a Komblo song alluding to their tardiness in getting their own Festival dancing under way by comparison with Sekaka dancers across the river, and to the fact that when Komblo dancers *were* ready, rain prevented them from dancing:

> Mu gur dom, na pilye mei
> Tapi gur dom, na kane mei
> Pop to de de
> Kupo kerem, na kane mei
> Pop to de de

> I hear *mu* wood [from which drums are made] thunder
> I see *tapi* wood [also used for drum-making] resounding
> Clouds descend, I [still] watch.

The goal of the dancing is to attract courting partners to the performers, to overawe spectators from rival and enemy clans with the numbers, wealth and power of the dancers, and in so doing, to deter them from aggression. Dancing is sometimes described as 'building a fence around the land', and clansmen stress to each other how important it is that they should all participate – particularly on major occasions when dancers from other clans may visit to dance competitively alongside. Such dances, where the number of spectators may run into thousands, represent the peak of Wahgi visual performance (pl. 6). The spectators assess the number of men on display, the condition of their 'skin' (which should glint, glow and dazzle, not look dull or flaky), their dancing and other aspects of their performance.[19]

However, the capacity to mount compelling performances is also regarded as evidence of the *moral* condition of the performing group, both as far as clansmen's relations with each other are concerned, and vis-à-vis other clans. For the Wahgi, appearance is felt to be continuous with underlying moral status, rather than concealing it. As with the patterns of death and infertility described earlier, the dancers' appearance is scanned by spectators for evidence of concealed betrayals, hidden anger, and inter-clan indebtedness, all of which are thought to reveal themselves in affecting the condition of the dancers' skin. There are further parallels. Just as it is feared that a disaffected clansman may betray his fellows in warfare through covertly handing over some article to an enemy group, so it is thought that a man may sabotage his own group's dancing performance through delivering to rivals an item of adornment, or simply as a consequence of his concealed anger. Equally, it is only through the deed being brought to public knowledge that (it is felt) its damaging consequences can be halted. Important dances are preceded by long discussions during which those participating talk through their internal relationships, confessing grievances.

Among the issues thus considered by Kekanem and Anzkanem clans in their dancing for the 1970s Pig Festival were the troubling deaths and other episodes which had occurred over the preceding decades. As newly split (and therefore quite small) clans, Kekanem and Anzkanem had a common dance ground and generally danced as a single formation, but they did not always feel that their dancing was going well. One of the factors discussed as potentially responsible was the possibility that undisclosed anger still remained over Anzkanem's clubbing of Kekanem Simbil a generation earlier. Another related to the much more recent killing of Jiruka Aipe. My Kekanem sponsor, Kinden, is 'born of a Jiruka woman' and classed Aipe as one of his mother's close brothers, regarding him as a major 'source' person. On Aipe's death, Kinden had attempted to organise a supportive payment to Aipe's sons but many of Kinden's clansmen preferred to assist Aipe's killers, to whom *they* were related. Angry at their refusal to assist him, Kinden secretly visited Aipe's sons during their dancing to decorate them: rubbing pork fat onto their skins, inserting his own plumes into their headnets. It was these actions, Kinden later confessed, which lay behind the poor Kekanem and Anzkanem performance. Again, when visited by dancers from Kurup-Maiamka, Kekanem ritually invoked the latter's failure to reciprocate for all the brides they had received decades earlier from Kekanem refugees, an invocation aimed at sabotaging the effectiveness of the visitors' performance.

Just before the end of the Festival, the men of the performing clan erect one of two ritual structures near the centre of their ceremonial ground. It is around these ritual structures that the pigs will be killed and in many ways they are a key to what the Festival is about. One of these ritual structures is the short decorated *mond* post. This appears to be an older form, and is being displaced by the second type of structure, the miniature *bolyim* house, a ritual innovation which is spreading westward from its origin amongst Simbu groups. In their previous Pig Festivals, Komblo clans had always erected *mond* posts. However, for the Festival that climaxed in 1980, three of the four main Komblo clans decided to erect *bolyim* houses instead. To do so, as earlier recorded, representatives from the Komblo clans in question returned to their original Narku homeland in Simbu Province. There, in coded talk, they asked to acquire the rights and knowledge to erect the *bolyim* house, the ritual form they see themselves as having left behind when first they fled. Instructors came from Narku to teach the three acquiring clans how to construct *bolyim* houses and the associated taboos. (It was partly because they feared that there were no men prepared to shoulder these onerous taboos that the fourth main Komblo clan, Kekanem, decided against acquiring *bolyim*.)

Despite their rather different external appearance, and some variation in

Fig. 2 1 'Source people' must be paid, if the children of a marriage are to thrive (1990).

the accompanying ritual, the *mond* post and *bolyim* house are, in structural terms, identical. Ideologically, they can be seen as putting forward the same claim: briefly that an immortal, male clan is the self-sufficient source of its own fertility and growth. Consider the following: [i] of all the components of the Pig Festival, it is the *bolyim* house and *mond* post which are particularly felt to promote future growth and fertility amongst pigs and people: it is they which are erected at the climax to the Festival at the centre of the ceremonial ground; it is they which are anointed and topped with pork fat; [ii] both *bolyim* house and *mond* post are represented as invulnerable to time. For at the end of the Pig Festival, they are dismantled and their timbers re-buried in a swampy spot where they remain until the next Pig Festival, when they are excavated and re-erected: and it is always emphasised that no matter how long the timbers stay buried they will not decay; [iii] both *bolyim* house and *mond* post are male productions. They are erected secretly on the ceremonial ground at night (ideally by the sons of the men who did so at the clan's previous Pig Festival), while women (who know perfectly well what is happening) are banished to their houses; finally [iv] *bolyim* house and *mond* post *are* the clan, in the sense that a clan erects either one or the other, and both are described as modelling the clan in their structure. For example, each of the three twists of *banz* vine projecting from the top of Kekanem's *mond* post was said to stand for one of the main Kekanem subgroups, whilst the same was said of the four wallposts supporting Anzkanem's *bolyim* house.

What this series of identifications does is to attach the attributes of fertility, growth, immortality, and maleness to the clan, to make them properties of it. Notable is what is thereby omitted. Time's impact on the clan, registered in the variable processes of fission and shrinkage, is glossed over. Wives' contribution to clan fertility and growth in the form of bearing children and raising pigs is disregarded. In particular, other clans' contributions, as the providers of wives and among whom 'source' people are consequently to be found, are overlooked. The thrust of a number of the Festival rituals is, in fact, precisely to mark off the performing clan from others. All this returns us to the tension initially observed to be at the heart of Wahgi society: between loyalties owed to clan, and those an individual owes to 'source people' beyond the clan. What the Pig Festival 'does' as a ritual, partly through the agency of *bolyim* house and *mond* post, is to present the performing clan as the autonomous and self-sufficient source of its own growth and fertility. In doing so, the Festival momentarily denies what in other circumstances is acknowledged: that the clan is actually constituted of external assets – the wives marrying in from outside – and that purportedly united clansmen are (as we have seen) divided by the loyalties they each individually owe to their respective external 'sources'.

The longer-term future of the Festival is, however, in doubt, with few if any Festivals being performed in the Wahgi since the Komblo and Sekaka ones. To some degree, the demands of coffee-growing and the intensive pig husbandry required by the Festival are in conflict. Though coffee income provides many of the plumes needed for Festival dancing, coffee trees have reduced the available acreage of pig pasture. During their late 1970s Festival, many Komblo grumbled that the event was too protracted, and there was a sense that this would be the last one they would perform. The necessity to assert clan strength and numbers in the face of surrounding enemies was also partly undercut by the dramatic peace-making which I describe below. Sub-

Fig. 22 Contemporary dress, including netbags made from acrylic yarn (1990).

sequently, though, Komblo have been less sure; listening, years later, to my tapes of their dancing, some spoke as though it was only a matter of time before a new Festival was inaugurated.

'Becoming one'

The concluding and most spectacular events of the Komblo Pig Festival took place early in January 1980. Men of each clan, supported by their allies, charged onto their dance ground and circled the ritual structures at its centre, before climbing on to the *bolyim* house and on to specially-erected platforms. There, as earlier noted, they ate great quantities of pork fat in front of thousands of spectators, imprinting on them an image (one that I have suggested is distinctly partial) of the Festival-holding clan as the united source of its own wealth and strength, of a group 'at the height of their communal existence' (cf A.J. Strathern 1985:127). On 14 January, the pigs (some 700 of them) were killed – and then immediately afterwards a new era was abruptly inaugurated: Komblo and the coalition of their enemies who had ousted them in warfare fifty years earlier formally made peace, 'becoming one'.

Komblo men often presented the initiative to make peace as actually coming from their former opponents who, it was asserted, had been overwhelmed by the numbers and appearance of Komblo dancers during the Pig Festival. However, Komblo themselves were also undoubtedly moved towards reconciliation by a claustrophobic sense of having been hemmed in by enemies for half a century. Economic motives were no less significant. Komblo businessmen such as Yimbal and Tai, who had begun to rent or purchase stores in the 'enemy' town of Banz and elsewhere, were acutely aware that their enterprises would be vulnerable in any future outbreak of fighting and for this reason wished to make peace formally. Equally vulnerable were those, such as my sponsor Kinden, who had purchased shares in local coffee plantations or other concerns. Kinden also relates the prominent role he took in the peace-making to his own earlier wide-ranging activities promoting the Savings and Loans Society, which had brought him into contact with established figures amongst enemy groups, such as Kulaka Mek and Kumnika Moli. Both these men had in fact visited the platform on which Kinden consumed pork at the climax to the Pig Festival. There, in defiance of the taboo on enemies sharing food, they accepted beer from him, an act to which the subsequent peace-making is also traced.

Before it was considered safe to make peace, however, the taboos segregating the two sides had to be undone. A week after the end of the Pig Festival, Komblo gathered in small groups to wash their hands in water containing *gowul* and *alap* leaves which ritually remove the charcoal of warfare, and cool the heat of fighting; *omb mang*, a variety of sugar cane, was chewed and the spittings were deposited in the Kar River to be carried away. Over the next fortnight, with the separating taboos thus shed, Komblo subgroups formally ate together with most of the clans with whom they had fought. These were poignant occasions, as relatives sundered for fifty years embraced in tears, mutually urging each other to eat from the same food, in some instances actually having to be introduced to each other. Groups of mission adherents – who took the role of 'path' or 'source people' in bringing the sides together

– prayed energetically over them. This was also a more general peace-making, attempting to bring to an end divisions within Komblo itself: Jiruka Aipe's sons ate with his killers.

Then on 5 February, Komblo clansmen climbed their Ongmange fastness formally to uproot the tokens which they had covertly been given over the years by disaffected clansmen from among their enemies. As earlier noted, these tokens, buried under hardwood stakes or taking the form of growing plants, had been intended to benefit Komblo in any subsequent fighting. Komblo now burned them, thus partially disarming themselves. As each token was thrown on the fire, the name of the group, some member of which had smuggled the item into Komblo hands, was called aloud. Burned, too, were the durable markers which Komblo individuals themselves had buried as testament to their own determination to revenge themselves for specific deaths.

The ritual of peace-making culminated in a major ceremony organised by the Catholic Church. It was held in the local town of Banz, on which Komblo and their erstwhile enemies converged in thousands on 16 February 1980. A dais, ornamented with Papua New Guinean flags, had been constructed. On it stood Father Peter, the long-serving Catholic priest in the area, along with Catholic Sisters and politicians. They were joined by spokesmen from the two sides who each took hold of one end of a spear preserved from the fighting and snapped it (pl. 10). Komblo and their former opponents were referred to as united like the paired halves of a single plume from a Princess Stephanie bird of paradise. Older men from the two sides were asked to approach the dais in pairs, where they were jointly given a mouthful of liver or pork.

It was almost as though the two sides were being married – and, in fact, within a few weeks marriages and other long-delayed payments between the two sides were resumed (see fig. 7). There was a feeling that a new era was beginning, or had at least been legitimised. In some ways time *had* in a sense been frozen while the tokens of each side's determination to inflict revenge on the other remained hidden and active, like unconfessed anger. These tokens are after all invulnerable to time, either buried under hardwood stakes or comprising such plants as cordylines, which renew themselves. But with their uprooting and burning, and the ceremony of eating together, time was symbolically re-started, under the new order of church and state, embodied in the priest and the Papua New Guinean flags on the dais. It was noteworthy that in their speeches at this time men from both sides emphasised that they were really 'offspring of mission and Administration', of a different generation from their fathers who had borne the bulk of the 1920s fighting. Equally, while the meal at the dais comprised the traditional liver and pork, people had often remarked during their earlier meetings on the fact that it was new foods that they were now sharing: tea and coffee, bread, biscuits and soft drinks. There was talk too of finding a new joint name (Konzka) for the two sides, of reducing the size of compensation payments which a driver's clan is expected to pay to that of an accident victim, and of abolishing the aggressive style of presentation of such payments.

There were also indications of adjustments to thinking on matters of ghostly causation. When Kekanem, returning from one of the commensal occasions, found that in their absence Pilei's young son Bamne had cut himself severely with an axe they did not attribute this to ghostly disapproval of their eating with enemies, but rather to Pilei's own failure to attend the event. The deaths of two Monglka men at the time were equally laid at the door of their obstinate refusal to participate in the peace-making.

Yet it would not do to overemphasise this shift. For all the holy water that was poured on the tokens before uprooting them for burning, men expressed nervousness at the possible ghostly consequences of their destruction. And when Kekanem men returned from burning the tokens they found elderly Pulndam, brother of the slain Kekanem warrior Tai, mute and unmoving in his house. The spear which he had held as a token to revenge his brother's death had been taken and destroyed without his knowledge, and he was apparently worried that he would be attacked by his brother's ghost. Nor did everyone eat with the enemy coalition: those responsible for erecting the *bolyim* house and *mond* post were not permitted to do so. Others commented that some items of war-magic still remained hidden, and the very fact that details of former killings were now more accessible generated further disputes as people learned more of the circumstances under which their kin had been slain.

Contemporary warfare

A further motive behind this local effort to inaugurate a new era of cooperation and peace was the fact that warfare had indeed resumed in parts of the Highlands. Since the early 1970s, quite large-scale battles, sometimes lasting weeks and months, and involving considerable damage to property and loss of life, have taken place between clans and tribes in a number of the Highlands provinces. First the Australian colonial authorities, and subsequently the Papua New Guinean national government, endeavoured to counter this with a battery of reports and legislation, including the formation of specialist mobile riot squads. Nevertheless, the level of fighting escalated to the point that a state of emergency was declared in all five Highlands provinces in July 1979. This was quite effective, at least temporarily, as also were subsequent local initiatives, such as the founding by the Western Highlands Provincial Government of a Peace and Good Order Committee (Mell 1988). Philip Kapal, the Province's premier, described the Committee as an attempt to use local cultural practices of mediation and compensation to settle local problems. The Committee comprises prominent men, known for their compelling speech-making, who are conveyed to the site of actual or potential scenes of conflict where they endeavour to persuade the participants to compromise. Wahgi members of the Committee include both Kumnika Moli and also my sponsor Kinden (fig. 23), for whom membership is the latest in a long list of activities aimed at preventing a recurrence of warfare, feared as much for its effects on *bisnis* as for the trauma of refugeeship.

Despite such initiatives, the fighting has proved refractory. In places, it has become more rather than less severe, since the traditional armoury of bows and arrows, spears and axes has been complemented since the mid-1980s by the addition of guns. Most of these are 'home-mades', firing shotgun cartridges from sections of piping strapped to a wooden stock (fig. 24); occasionally, manufactured rifles, either stolen from the police or, it is said, acquired

Fig. 23 Kekanem Kinden, wearing card identifying him as a member of the local Peace Committee. He also wears P.N.G.'s 10th Anniversary of Independence medal and Land Mediator's insignia (1990).

from neighbouring Irian Jaya, are also used.[20] Efforts to quell the fighting have also been complicated by the fact that today higher level units are drawn into disputes which might once have been handled at a clan or tribal level: what A.J. Strathern (1992:230) calls the 'tribalization' of these higher level units. Komblo had partly anticipated this, advancing as a further reason for finally making peace with their neighbours their concern that the northwest Wahgi as a whole might get embroiled in fighting against equivalently large units elsewhere.

The events which followed the killing of Seth Timano illustrate the way in which more encompassing political units can be drawn into disputes. Seth Timano, a businessman from Enga Province, was shot by a dozen men from the Mt. Hagen area of the Western Highlands Province in August 1990. I am not clear whether the shooting resulted from an earlier dispute between those involved, or was carried out by one of the gangs of robbers, known as *raskol*, which have emerged as a threat to order along with inter-group warfare. Whichever was the case, the way in which the ensuing compensation claims were phrased is significant. According to a press report,[21] the relatives of Mr Timano demanded K22,000 and 500 pigs from each of the suspects' clans. But this was completely overshadowed by the demand served by a delegation from Enga Province upon the Western Highlands Government itself for K1 million and 5,000 pigs. Rumours that convoys of men from Enga were descending upon Mt. Hagen to press this claim led to the town substantially shutting down on the days in question, since considerable damage had followed a previous such invasion, itself the consequence of the killing of another Engan man on an earlier occasion. This contemporary tendency for disputes

Fig. 24 Confiscated 'home-mades', Banz police station (1990).

to develop an inter-province dimension was further highlighted when a Western Highlands student, but this time from Wahgi rather than Hagen, was killed in a brawl with Enga students at the University of Papua New Guinea in Port Moresby shortly after Mr Timano's death.

A wide range of causes have been educed to explain the 'revival' of Highlands warfare (see Knauft 1990). The Highlands provinces are among the most densely populated areas of the country. Consequently, some commentators have stressed land shortage, aggravated by continuing population increase and the demands of cash-cropping, as a major cause. Gordon and Meggitt (1985) have argued that land shortage as a factor should be seen in conjunction with the effects of administrative changes, whereby 'generalist' patrol officers were replaced by a plethora of specialised law and order agencies which proved to be less effective in settling disputes and catching and convicting offenders. Others have seen the fighting as part of a struggle for local supremacy by powerful leaders attempting to destroy their rivals among neighbouring groups. Some accounts further suggest that those in the front line are landless and unemployed youths being manipulated by such leaders, and interpret the fighting, and *raskol* activities more generally, as social protest against increasing inequalities in the Highlands (Good 1979:120-1; see also Sillitoe 1978).

From a Wahgi perspective, the first point to make is that fighting had never completely died away. Despite Corrigan's earlier obituary for warfare, a patrol officer was noting in the mid-1950s, for example, that 'the North Wahgi area has been the scene of numerous fights between individuals, and at times between subgroups and groups'.[22] Komblo, for instance, engaged in a major invasion of their Sekaka neighbours at this time, though they did not deploy shields, whose use was traditionally one of the marks of full-scale warfare.

53

It would be false, then, to draw an absolute contrast between decades of colonial peace and the present situation; in fact, as A.J. Strathern (1977:143) has observed, the exchanges and ceremonies which effloresced during the colonial period also functioned to keep alive the structure of older enmities which often stoke contemporary conflicts.

A second point is that any explanation has to take into account the fact that, where recent warfare has taken place in the Wahgi, it has only done so in particular areas. It is around Minj that fighting has been heaviest, particularly involving Konumbka, Kondika, Ngeneka, Koleka and Tangilka groups (map 2). In the centre of the valley, Senglap and Dange fought in 1989, as did Kurupka and Maiamka at Kudjip in 1992. In contrast, Komblo, Kumnika, Sekaka and Kulaka, the old antagonists in the northwest Wahgi area, have not warred recently. Furthermore, where fighting has occurred, combatants have often voluntarily limited their use of weaponry, a point I discuss in the next chapter with respect to changes in shield technology.

Third, it is clear that economic inequality is indeed growing in the Wahgi and is likely to become increasingly entrenched, both through processes of wealth inheritance and as a result of differential educational opportunities. Yimbal and Tai, for example, now own businesses with a total turnover of many thousands of Kina, and have also begun to buy land elsewhere in the valley. It is not difficult to foresee circumstances in which such accumulation might lead to discontent and perhaps to violence. This is, in fact, a point well recognised by Yimbal, who pursues a deliberate policy of converting economic bonds into moral ones by endeavouring to forge linking marriages between his clan and the groups in whose territory he buys land or establishes businesses. Yimbal, who himself has seven wives, referred to such marriages in Pidgin as 'strongim' the relationship. He also commented that the offspring of the marriages would always be in a position to inform him if problems were brewing: a contemporary use of the special relationship with 'source people'.

It is equally possible to envisage that competition between leaders in the northwest Wahgi area might, at some point in the future, be expressed in inter-clan fighting. To date, however, the inverse has been much more striking. Partly because their investments are distributed in such a way as to make them vulnerable in the event of warfare, wealthy leaders have tended to promote reconciliation rather than the reverse – a point which emerged in the earlier discussion of Komblo's peace-making. In fact, some leaders in the northwest Wahgi area are alleged to have handed over tokens which would undermine their respective clans' capacities in warfare, in an effort to prevent fighting. What also seems likely, however, is that once warfare *does* break out, the ensuing destruction of businesses and coffee trees makes it increasingly difficult for participants to raise the wealth necessary to settle the issue through compensation.

Over the course of this chapter I have tried to embed a sketch of Wahgi material culture in the context of a developing Wahgi history, giving as much weight to contemporary artefacts such as vehicles, money and beer as to stone axes, spears and shells. In the next chapter I focus on particular material forms in more detail, now looking at them from the point of view of making a collection.

CHAPTER TWO

Collecting in context

This chapter aims to provide more material on the artefacts whose cultural and historical context was described in the previous chapter, and which feature in the exhibition. In particular, it describes contemporary netbags and shields, the best represented of the artefacts on display. Both exemplify the complexities of continuity, transformation and re-contextualisation which emerged in the account of Komblo's history and that of the Wahgi more generally.

However, as a device for providing material on the artefacts, I sketch some of the processes involved in collecting them. This is partly to make the account less dry than it might otherwise be, but partly also because the process of making a collection itself proved to be more interesting than I had naively expected. It confronted me with my own taken-for-granted assumptions as to the nature of the transactions I was engaged in, the definition of 'material culture', and what actually constituted a 'Wahgi artefact'. Collecting also proved to be more complex than its rather one-dimensional contemporary reputation, sketched in the Introduction, would suggest. As I noted there, I did not find myself a free agent, assembling a collection according to my own whim. I discovered that my collecting was constrained by local processes and rules, with the upshot that the collection I made partly mirrored in its own structure local social organisation. And while many comments on collecting have focused upon the 'rupture' involved in removing artefacts from their local context to install them in the rather different one of a museum or gallery, this was not necessarily the way in which the Wahgi themselves chose to view the matter.

Perhaps one reason for the rather negative stereotype recently enjoyed by collecting has to do with our own culture's particular view of money and transactions which involve it. As Parry and Bloch (1989) have pointed out, we have tended to fetishise money, to conceive of it as a powerfully invasive force which necessarily depersonalises and commercialises the bonds of sentiment and morality we regard as characteristic of small-scale communities. Certainly, before leaving for the Wahgi, I did feel moments of unease at the notion of returning to the community I had lived in as an anthropologist, but now with the intention of purchasing artefacts for removal.

Yet, as I ought to have remembered, the distinction between 'sentiment' and 'money' which underlay my disquiet is not universal. Social relationships in the Highlands are not regarded as somehow depersonalised because money, or other goods, have passed between those involved: indeed, it is through such exchanges that relationships are formed and maintained.[1] And if my removing anything from the community caused unease, it had been in the context of my original work as an anthropologist, when I had been accused of wandering in the graveyard, siphoning off intangible ancestral power – behaviour felt to be witchlike. Removing the collection at the end of my stay *was* re-categorised in local terms: but now one implication was that I was in the position less of a witch than of an in-law, owing the payments due to 'source people'.

These points are not made in an attempt to invert a stereotype: to suggest that, contrary to much recent characterisation, ethnographic collecting is always a 'good' thing. My intention is merely to point out that it is a widely engaged-in activity which lately has been more judged than described; and that, in the particular circumstances in which I engaged in it, it proved to be somewhat at odds with its image, and to offer unexpected sidelights.[2]

However, a month before I went to the Highlands, the Highlands came to London. In the early summer of 1990, the organisation Cultural Cooperation arranged a European tour for a contingent of Papua New Guinean dancers, including a group from Mt. Hagen. At every venue, the different groups each decorated and danced in their local styles. I want to describe briefly the performance they gave in Gunnersbury Park in West London (fig. 25), partly to demonstrate the interconnectedness between events in London

Fig. 25 The New Guinea Highlands in West London: Hagen women dance in Gunnersbury Park (1990).

and the apparently distant New Guinea Highlands, and partly as an example of the way such events may be re-contextualised by the media. Despite the chilly June weather, the dancers performed in the open, where their displays seemed appreciated by the British crowds who came to see them. Indeed, many spectators participated in the final dance, a Hagen one known as *mørli*, which involves the performers linking arms and dancing round in a circle. As a spectator, I found the occasion somewhat vertiginous, in the way it bridged realms seemingly quite remote from each other. *Mørli*, for example, is a dance which in-married Hagen wives have taught Komblo, and I had last seen it done during the intense final months of the Komblo Pig Festival. To see it done next by enthusiastic crowds of West Londoners against the classical façade of Gunnersbury House, was disorienting; as was encountering among the dancers one of the members of the Simbu party who had sold the *bolyim* house to Komblo clans a decade before.

Much odder to any Hageners who subsequently watched it would have seemed the way their performance was presented on television.[3] The item featuring the dancers was introduced by the presenter who peered out of the Gunnersbury Park shrubbery, warning viewers that:

> Out in the wilds of West 4 a strange tribe have been located. The Melpa [Hagen] people from New Guinea may look primitive but ladies, cop this: not only do the blokes cook all their own meals but there is a deeply held belief in pre-marital chastity [and here her tone of voice became arch] for the men!

The presenter then continued, as she pushed through the shrubbery, now conscripted into the role of jungle trail:

> Melpa people's first taste of the West was when they ate English missionaries. Performing at Gunnersbury Park as part of the New Guinea Festival, they are art on legs.

Amidst snatches of Hagen singing and dancing, she went on:

> Taking three hours to apply their exotic make-up and feathered costumes, the Melpa people make Joan Collins look under-dressed . . . Audiences be warned: hang on to your heads as well as your hats!

The item was remarkable for the economy with which the Hagen visitors were slotted into the 'cannibal natives eat missionaries in jungle' stereotype. What is particularly ironic is that far from ever having been cannibals, or killed missionaries, Hageners themselves (like the Wahgi) think of cannibalism as a definitively unnatural practice. No less intriguing, perhaps, is the bracketing of male premarital chastity, men cooking their own meals, and cannibalism as practices of equal oddity.

A month after the Gunnersbury event my wife and I moved into the house which Zacharias, Kinden's son, had built for us at Topkalap, the settlement where we had lived on previous visits to the Wahgi. Before I could make a start on the collection, however, one consequence of the New Guinea performers' European tour had to be defused. To my concern, there was a widespread expectation that my purpose in returning to the Highlands was to recruit a

Fig. 26 Wooden bowl in which Wahgi traditionally kneaded pandanus fruit to produce an oily food. 1990 Oc.9.542; L: 53 cm.

contingent of Wahgi dancers to tour Britain, just as their Hagen neighbours had done. Once I had done what I could to explain the situation, three further issues, at once practical and conceptual, had to be addressed: what exactly was I there to collect, how was collecting to be organised, and what should be paid for the artefacts collected?

At one level the answer to the first question was simple: 'Wahgi material culture'. That was certainly what I had indicated in my proposal to the Museum's Trustees, and I thought I knew what would be covered by the term. Though there is no precise Wahgi equivalent, what I had in mind was the full repertoire of portable Wahgi goods, including personal adornment of all kinds, clothing, netbags, household goods, weaponry. Possibly I could also commission a *bolyim* house and *mond* post. The emphasis was to be on completeness, with contemporary material, such as the contents of a trade-store, represented equally with traditional items.

Despite these catholic intentions, however, I found myself unthinkingly privileging as 'Wahgi' those items which were produced in the area, rather than merely used there. One instance of this arose from my wish to acquire a wooden pandanus processing bowl (fig. 26), a type of artefact displaced in most areas of the Wahgi by metal equivalents. At length, one Wahgi visitor to Topkalap brought what was said to be such a vessel: and produced for inspection what I was sure was a bowl made in the Sepik area for sale to tourists. My curatorial protests that this was not a *Wahgi* pandanus processing bowl were met with an equally firm assertion that it was. Belatedly, I realised that we were arguing at cross-purposes. For me, the bowl was ineligible on the grounds that it had been produced by a Sepik carver for sale to visitors; the seller's point was that this was a Wahgi pandanus processing bowl because (whatever its origins) it had been used by Wahgi to process pandanus, as indeed the oily stains testified. I regret now that I did not buy this, or a surprisingly wide range of other items flushed out of Wahgi houses by the opportunity to sell them but which nevertheless fell outside my somewhat puritan definition of 'Wahgi material culture'.

Raised in tandem with the issue of precisely what to buy was the problem of how to organise its purchase. The house at Topkalap had been intended as a base and had been constructed to a size capable of accommodating the collection. This however left unresolved the logistical question of whether the collection should be made through visiting settlements to buy artefacts there, or waiting for them to be brought to Topkalap. This is a dilemma to which Rena Lederman (1986:369) refers in her sensitive account of collecting information in the Southern Highlands. She found that the theoretically more desirable course – of herself travelling to meet people in their own settlements – was impractical: too much of her time was spent walking between settlements, and being made a guest when she arrived. I found the same conditions applied to collecting artefacts – with the added drawback that anything acquired would have to be carried home. The great majority of items purchased, then, were brought to Topkalap and offered for sale there.

This logistical matter related to another, potentially more delicate: who to buy artefacts from and in what order. Around the fieldwork house which he built for me and my wife on our first visit to the Wahgi in 1979, Kinden had created what he told me was a 'garden'; a short path led from the front door to the garden gate, which he ornamented with some large stones which formed a convenient ledge on which to retie boot laces. As I soon discovered, however, the point of the garden was as much the fence round it as the plants inside it, and the stones were those which traditionally mark the entrance to a taboo-ed area. The 'garden' was part of Kinden's attempt to reserve for himself and the community at Topkalap any benefits which might prove to flow from the gamble of lodging this odd White couple professing an interest in local culture. Understandably, the community did not see why others who had not taken the risk of doing so should benefit from the payments and gifts which we made in return for information; equally, I knew my work would suffer if I was restricted in that way. The early months of my first fieldwork were partly devoted to working out a mutually satisfactory compromise.

My return to Topkalap with money to spend on artefacts potentially raised this issue of the distribution of wealth in even sharper form. Although my collecting trip commenced in July, when there is a considerable amount of coffee income in circulation, the money which I had available to purchase artefacts and assistance still represented a substantial local asset. I worried that it might prove difficult to manage the tension between the demands of the immediate community, who would be likely to want me to buy exclusively from them, and my own wish to purchase a wider range of artefacts than they would be likely to possess. On this occasion, the local claims had the added force that we were also dependent on community protection from armed *raskol* gangs, a matter of some moment when the equivalent of thousands of pounds in cash had regularly to be transported and stored.

My concern was largely misplaced; Kinden proved to have quite clear ideas as to how to proceed. There should, he declared, be a specific order in which people should be entitled to offer artefacts for sale, particularly in the case of the most valuable category, netbags. First, people living in the local community at Topkalap should be asked, then the remainder of the subclans which make up Kekanem, then the paired clan of Anzkanem, then the other Komblo clans of Jiruka and Kulka, then Sekaka, the tribe across the Kar river, then other Wahgi. In fact this principle of structural distance did not rigidly govern subsequent transactions: some individuals from more distant groups, whom I happened to know well, took advantage of the fact to offer material in advance of their 'turn'; some artefacts, such as shields, were simply not available within Komblo; many structurally-close individuals came back more than once to offer items for sale.

Nevertheless, Kinden's scheme did broadly influence the proceedings, if only because he initially acted as master of ceremonies, selecting the order in which potential sellers presented themselves. I equally knew that it would be politically impossible to continue to reside within a community without giving them priority in offering material for sale. Certainly, these were the terms in which the odd objection was raised, with occasional individuals from within Komblo grumbling that I had been buying artefacts from enemies across the river when they themselves had yet to sell me anything. Correspondingly, the inhabitants of Topkalap worried periodically that the public flow of wealth in the settlement might provoke jealousy and witchcraft. Predictably, too, ordering the purchase of artefacts by corporate group at times ran up against the cross-cutting loyalties which individuals owe to 'source people'. Kapil, Kinden's wife's brother from Sekaka tribe, threatened to pronounce a lethal curse against his nephews and nieces at Topkalap if I did not purchase anything from him. The threat was tongue-in-cheek, but once I had bought something Kapil assured me that now they would 'thrive' (*para pa senda*), and the incident was an effective reminder of a tension at the heart of Wahgi society.

At the same time such processes also made the collection itself more interesting. While at one level it certainly reflected my own conception of what 'a collection of Wahgi material culture' should include, at another level the collection necessarily embodied local conditions and processes. The fact that it was constituted predominantly of Komblo artefacts reflected the *realpolitik* of field collecting, and the order in which the artefacts were acquired partially reproduced local social structure, including its characteristic tensions, seen from one community's perspective. While mine may be an extreme example, I suspect that most ethnographic collections contain much more of an indigenous ordering than their contemporary reputation – as having been assembled according to alien whim and 'torn' from a local context – often allows.

A final arena of cultural negotiation related to what should be given in return for artefacts acquired. For, of the dozens of people who gathered daily at Topkalap with artefacts to sell (fig. 27), only the occasional individual, generally non-Komblo, was willing to specify a price. 'It's up to you', they would say instead, and almost never demur at the sum I suggested. In some instances, this reflected a genuine uncertainty as to what a rarely transacted item might be worth. But at another level, reluctance to specify a price stemmed from the fact that the transactions were rarely purchases in any simple sense. They had as much the character of local exchanges, in which precise amounts are not necessarily worked out in advance. As such, what is given on either side is 'an evaluation by the persons of each other and not just a commercial transaction with generalised rates', as A.J. Strathern (1981:301) notes of his own transactions in purchasing food in Hagen, when he too was told that he should decide the amount that it was appropriate to pay.

In fact, I was not entirely without guidelines in suggesting prices. Some artefacts, such as items of adornment, are regularly offered for sale to other Wahgi in roadside markets, while others, such as netbags, are made for sale to tourists passing through Mt. Hagen airport. I took these, and the fact that

there was a continuous supply of sellers, as an indication that I was pitching things roughly right.

The fact that these were not simple purchases was highlighted by those sellers who explicitly situated the transaction in broader moral terms. Sometimes this would be done in terms of a clan, or corporate group, frame of reference. Thus a seller might tell me, when I asked him (I do not recall hearing a woman use this frame of reference) how much he wanted for an artefact, that both he and I were 'within' (*tuale*), with the implication that our membership of the same group made careful calculations of price inappropriate. Other sellers, related to my sponsor Kinden as 'source people', would co-opt me to the same relationship, and I would be told that I might give what I pleased, since 'we are as mother's brother and sister's child, not strangers', or 'like source people'. The transaction was thus re-defined not as a commercial matter but in terms of uncalculating exchange between kin. As I noted earlier, this kinship idiom was again to be evoked when I finally left with the collection. But it is important to recognise the potent charge which such disavowals of material interest carry. By overtly moving the transaction out of the commercial realm, they actually require a response equally free of cost-counting.

As people became clearer as to what I wanted to collect (once they had internalised my stereotype of their material culture), they began to become interested in the collection's contents and representativeness. Some speculated that it would not be possible to obtain such discontinued items as aprons ornamented with pigs' tails, or the plaited leg bands which women used to make as gifts for men. (Today men wear the ribbing from the tops of socks in place of the latter. For a long time I thought this was purely a modern fashion, not realising that sock-tops were a contemporary form of leg band.) Men began on their own initiative to make examples of abandoned categories of artefact, such as the parry shields traditionally used in the limited fighting permitted within the clan.

Fig. 27 Artefacts (eel trap and storage containers, shields) lined up for purchase outside author's house at Topkalap; 'taboo stones' to right (1990).

Fig. 28 Making *geru* boards for museum collection. Gum from the fruit (right) is used to stick strips of banana leaf to the board, like a stencil. Once the board has been painted the strips are removed, leaving a sharp-edged geometrical design; seated l-r Pilei, Anamb, Paiye (1986).

Other artefacts, for example the *geru* boards believed to promote pig growth and to alleviate sickness, I knew I would have to commission. Unlike parry shields, *geru* boards are still occasionally produced, but they are ephemeral artefacts and are not preserved after the end of the ceremony for which they are made. Commissioned artefacts have, perhaps, a reputation in museums of being somewhat ersatz, inferior to items hallowed by local use. Yet if one goal of making a field collection is to obtain the fullest possible information about the significance of the objects being collected, the artificial process of commissioning them may, paradoxically, be the most effective way of achieving it. The production and wearing of *geru*, for example, is hedged around with restrictions. The boards are made in seclusion and, while they are under construction, their wearer-to-be must avoid any contact with enemies; 'source people', on the other hand, *should* visit the wearer and make him or her a gift indicative of their goodwill, if the board is to appear bright and vivid as it should.

I knew all this from my earlier fieldwork, but the knowledge had only been acquired slowly, during the course of many discussions and while watching dozens of *geru* boards being made for local use. For rules such as these are not likely to be enunciated: they are simply part of the background knowledge against which an activity proceeds. The making of commissioned *geru* boards for a museum collection (fig. 28) was a different matter. Because it was artificial, all the rules surrounding *geru* board production were proclaimed – but in the form of jokes. Passers-by were pressed into walk-on parts. 'Don't come any nearer', the *geru*-board maker would call out to some matron trudging home under a netbag of sweet potatoes, 'women from enemy clans must keep away'. Other passers-by were jokingly hailed as 'source people' coming to make a gift to the *geru*-wearer as a token of their goodwill. An afternoon spent in this way, watching an item being made for sale, confirmed far more about its local significance than twice the time spent watching the 'real' thing.

I also found that the practicalities entailed in making a collection of artefacts revealed complexities which I had not previously appreciated. Sometimes, these were minor social and technical details which I had observed before but never really *seen*: the counter-intuitive techniques for storing the long black Stephanie plumes; the propensity for a man's apron belt to become trapped under a girlfriend's leg when engaged in stylised *man ngo* courting, resulting in a discomfort which it is impossible to relieve as it is taboo for a courting couple to mention words with sexual connotations like 'apron'; the tendency of apparently robust spears to bow if not supported when stored.

At other times, collecting highlighted variations among Wahgi themselves in their approach to artefacts. Kulka Kolnga, for example, had preserved intact from the 1960s his share of shell valuables received from two bridewealth payments. Where other individuals had disposed of most of their shells as they fell out of fashion, or had burned them to make lime to be eaten with betel nut, Kolnga secreted his, a strategy which paid off in the end since he disposed of them to me as a collection. The unusually crowded interior of his house, packed with cardboard boxes and other items, suggested that shells were not the only things he was reluctant to dispose of. Strictly speaking, I suspect Kolnga's assemblages are closer to 'accumulations' than to 'collections'. They appeared to lack one defining feature of collections: that of being assembled with particular classificatory principles in mind (Pearce 1992:49). Perhaps the item with regard to which the Wahgi do most closely exemplify collecting behaviour in this sense is not artefactual at all. It lies in the close interest they take in learning, evaluating and secreting accounts of past indebtedness and betrayal: factors which are felt to determine health, strength and fertility in the future.

On occasion, collecting artefacts threw up points entirely new to me. While I did know that Wahgi men, like many other Highlanders, consider women to be polluting in certain respects, I had not realised that skirts were potentially defiling, or that washing rid them of their polluting qualities (worried women told me that my 'skin' would become 'ashy' if I handled unwashed skirts). Nor did I realise that the fibres from which skirts are made might be re-worked to make netbags (fig. 29), but that it was cause for divorce for a wife to feed her husband with food which had been transported in such a netbag.

In addition to this somewhat anonymous way in which artefacts illustrate aspects of Wahgi culture, I was also interested in their capacity to embody something of the specific history of groups and individuals portrayed in Chapter 1. In some Papua New Guinean cultures, there exist highly significant ceremonial objects which are valued as a record of regional history – for instance, the armshells and necklaces which circulate in the celebrated *kula* exchange system in the Massim and evoke the names of the prominent individuals who have in the past possessed them. Some Highlands cultures also possess artefacts which stand for the structural continuity of society as a whole

Fig. 29 Netbag made from synthetic yarn, re-spun from an old skirt. 1990 Oc.9.83; w: 38.5 cm.

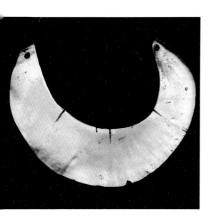

Fig. 30 The reverse of a pearl shell neck ornament; the incisions were made by the owner's husband who planned to cut it up for a shell belt. 1990 Oc.9.220; w: 20.5 cm.

(as *bolyim* house and *mond* post purport to do for a Wahgi clan[4]). The histories I had in mind, rather, were less grand ones, revealing instead something of the complexity of local stories and personal circumstance.

Let me give a single example: the *kine* shell ornament offered me by Kenzamb, the widow of the Kulka man, Ye Ka. It is an unexceptional shell, remarkable only for possessing a number of cuts on its reverse (fig. 30). As always, I asked Kenzamb how she had acquired it. Originally, she said, it had belonged to her father, Kowl. It had, in fact, been among the valuables he had concealed in her netbag when the besieged Komblo fled their Ongmange fastness in the early 1930s. Subsequently, her father had given the shell to her elder sister to wear while courting, and it had then passed to Kenzamb herself. The cuts on the shell's reverse had later been made by her husband, Ye Ka (though Kenzamb would not utter his name, for to name the dead is to risk invoking them). He had been in the process of breaking the ornament up to make a shell belt for the Pig Festival dancing, but Kenzamb stopped him in mid-course. Pursuing the history of this shell throws up details of cultural practices which might not otherwise emerge: the concealing of valuables in children's netbags; an instance of inheritance of a shell from an older sister; the taboo on uttering a dead husband's name; the purposive breaking of shell ornaments to provide the raw material for a belt; and a wife's capacity to prevent her husband doing this.[5]

I now want to look in more detail at two categories of artefact in particular: shields and netbags.

Battle shields[6]

The main Wahgi defensive weapon is the large plank-like war shield. Unlike the narrow parry shield, its use is restricted to serious warfare. In the past, it seems that the majority of men involved in a battle carried such shields, though some are said to have relied on their natural agility to avoid arrows and spears. My impression is that rather fewer shields are used in contemporary fighting, perhaps in part because weaponry is sometimes captured and destroyed by the Riot Squad. Lost shields cannot be replaced immediately, since the wood from which they are made must be allowed to dry if it is not to split upon being struck with spears or axes.

Traditionally, a shield would be made from a single plank of the outer wood of the *tapi* tree: *kumbtapi*, the term for a shield, literally means '*tapi* wall'. Although *tapi* (*Albizia* sp.) is a quick-growing tree and its wood is not heavy, the average shield made from it still weighs around 9kg. Wahgi men sometimes assert that it is the ancestral assistance which they invoke before a battle which enables them to manoeuvre for long periods carrying their shields over rugged ground. *Tapi* trees themselves are regarded as having a presiding spirit[7] which may also be invoked in time of war. There are no specialist shield-makers, and shields are generally made by those who intend to use them. Once the *tapi* tree has been felled, a length of trunk roughly the height of a man is separated, and wedges used to split off thick, longitudinal slabs of outer wood. These are then held over a fire to help dry them, before being pinned in a vice which prevents them from curling and cracking.

Once dry, the wood is trimmed and sand-papered with rough *kosong* leaves. Along the top of the shield a vine may be threaded through a series of small holes to help anchor the cassowary plumes, mounted on springy stems, which nod above the shield (fig. 31). The centre of the shield is pierced and a vine rope passed through the holes; this rope secures a sling which is looped over the left shoulder (assuming the carrier is right-handed) to support the shield's weight. A tough cane mesh is added to reinforce the vine rope on the exterior, where an axe blow might otherwise sever the rope and cause the shield to drop from the shoulder. Along the inner side of the shield, close to the right-hand edge, a further, thinner vine is attached, running vertically. The shield-carrier slots his left thumb through the lower end of this. Between them, shoulder sling and thumb string provide a sensitive mechanism for manipulating the shield, allowing it to be swivelled to cover front or rear, dropped sharply to protect the feet from an arrow, or elbowed away to counter a vigorous spear thrust which threatens to penetrate the shield and skewer the bearer. Conversely, this sensitivity is said to mean that an experienced warrior can gauge from the angle at which an opponent's shield is being held whether its bearer is about to advance or retreat (Muke, personal communication). Thus while a shield at one level conceals the body, it may also reveal the intentions of the carrier.

Before they are used in warfare, most shields are painted.[8] Traditionally, this was done using earth paints (which occur in reddish, white, tawny, and blue colours) and charcoal. Shield decoration, like shield-making, was not a specialist task and was generally undertaken by the owner who would draw upon the limited pool of Wahgi design elements to produce an individual result. Designs tend to be bilaterally symmetrical, and to be built up from elements based on the triangle, though the occasional shield may be painted black all over or left unadorned. The elements from which designs are assembled tend also to be large and bold: as Lowman (1973) has suggested for the quite similar Maring shields, this makes designs easier to see at a distance and perhaps enhances the impression made by warriors upon their opponents. Although the design elements are abstract in appearance, some at least are given names. These generally refer to the natural world: examples include 'bird's foot', 'heron's wing' or 'marsupial leg'. Occasionally, a design as a whole may be said to represent the human body, with a schematic head, arms and legs distinguished.

There seems, however, to be little significance to the design elements, at least at a conscious level. I have not, for example, heard Wahgi men link the different design motifs to any aspect of warfare, or say that the schematic representation of a man is terrifying to opponents, as the Wola do (Sillitoe 1980:495). If shield designs have any conscious significance for the Wahgi, it seems to be as a badge of individual identity. A number of men, when pressed as to the meaning of the motifs, commented that their designs allowed them to be recognised on the battlefield: both by their clansmen who could come to their aid if they saw they were in trouble, and by any 'source people' on the opposing side, who would know not to injure them.

Much of the foregoing derives, however, not from observation but from what I was told – for during my first period in the Wahgi at the end of the 1970s, I saw very few shields. They had either been abandoned or burned

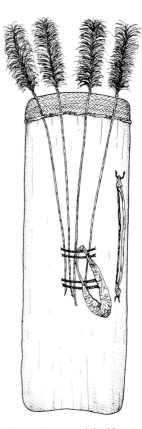

Fig. 31 Reverse of shield, showing cassowary plumes and support mechanism.

Fig. 32 Wooden shield; Dange tribe. Loosely, the inscription means 'Now buddy slays buddy'; 1990 Oc.9.20; H: 159.5 cm.

during colonial times. But as localised inter-group fighting increased during the 1980s, shields were made once again in parts of the Wahgi. While a few shields were similar to those of forty years before, many exhibited differences – underlying which were also continuities not always apparent at first sight. Some of the changes were technological. The replacement of stone axes by steel led many men to feel that the older cane mesh was no longer sufficient to protect the shoulder sling mounting from an axe blow; stouter materials (often pieces of metal) were therefore substituted for cane mesh. Then the introduction of home-made guns into the warfare in the Minj area after 1986 led some men there to experiment with all-metal shields. Made either from the cabin roofs of vehicles, or from 44 gallon drums, these were capable of stopping the charges of shotgun pellets which had penetrated a number of the wooden shields, wounding the men behind.

Contemporary shields differ also in their designs. First, these tend to be applied in durable oil paints rather than the traditional ochre. Secondly, designs today often incorporate varying amounts of lettering. Quite frequently, this is in the form of the date of the conflict. In one instance, the date given on the shield was not the year in which the conflict actually occurred but rather the following year (1990), thus anticipating the duration of the war. The scale of conflict was also registered on a further shield, used in warfare near Minj, which bore the legend 'Third World War'. Inscriptions may also take the form of including the shield-carrier's name. In one way, of course, this is a development of the notion that the design serves to mark out the identity of the bearer.[9] This is clearest in the case of the shield purchased from the Konumbka man, Kunump (pl. 11). Furthermore, when Kunump's shield was captured during the fighting and used by the opposing side, Kunump's name was actually rubbed out: reinforcing the point that shield design marks out the individuality of the shield carrier.

Written inscriptions parallel non-written forms in other respects too. For example, something of the same passionate regret as Ngunzka men expressed over the splitting of the clan following Simbil's killing (Chapter 1) seemed reflected in a shield used by Dange (see map 2) in the war against their Senglap neighbours. This shield (fig. 32) was inscribed around the boss with the Pidgin words '*Nau wantok kaikai wantok*' (loosely, 'Now buddy slays buddy'). Again, an inscription may be the written counterpart to the rejoinders traditionally made to a taunt (as, for example, Pig Festival holders dress one of their number as a woman in response to the taunt that they are 'like women'). In the case in question, a Konumbka youth inscribed his shield with the words '*Wagi pis*' ('Wahgi fish'). This was in rejoinder to an earlier taunt by Kondika opponents that they would force Konumbka back into the Wahgi river where their bodies would be consumed by fish.

Muke (personal communication) recalls seeing this last taunt inscribed on a shield, not in words but as a picture of a fish. This playing with words and images is also reflected in a set of shields which shows wider New Guinean idioms being put to local use. One such idiom is 'Six to Six'. This expression, which generally refers to a dusk to dawn party, has been incorporated into the design on the shields used by the Gilgalkup section of Senglap tribe. Its significance, however, has been inverted. Rather than referring to partying all night long, the expression was now said to be an assertion of Gilgalkup's ability to fight all day long.

These Gilgalkup shields raise a further point. While in the past, shield designs generally seem to have been specific to the individual warrior, members of three separate Senglap subgroups each explicitly co-ordinated their shield designs during their 1989 fighting against Dange. I was told that Senglap Gilgalkup all used 'Six 2 Six' shields (pl. 13), Senglap Baiman used shields based on an advertisement for South Pacific beer, while Senglap Olkanem all had 'Cambridge Cup' shields. This was not in fact entirely true. Though I saw only a selection of Senglap's shields, it was clear that at least the occasional man in the named subgroups had a shield whose decoration did not accord with that of the remainder of his subgroup. One reason given for this nonconformity returns us to the tension between loyalties owed to clan versus those to 'source people'. Thus Kaipel Ka, a Gilgalkup man whose own shield bore the South Pacific beer logo associated with Baiman (pl. 14), explained that as his mother's kin were Baiman he would sometimes fight alongside them, and so used the design otherwise associated with them.

Though the coordination of shield designs within subgroups is therefore only partial, and apparently limited to Senglap groups, it is still interesting to ask what may lie behind this shift towards uniformity. One important point is that two of the three co-ordinated sets of Senglap shields were decorated by the same individual, Kaipel Ka, mentioned above. Kaipel, a talented part-time sign-writer painted his fellow Senglap tribesmen's shields free or for nominal payment. In two instances, Kaipel also decorated the shields of relatives in other tribes: it was he who painted Kunump's shield, near the base of which he also discreetly advertised his sign-writing business at Talu (pl. 11, right).

But while Kaipel's expertise and possession of paints and brushes are obviously a factor, they cannot wholly account for this move toward co-ordinated design. An important background influence may well be the popularity of rugby league in Papua New Guinea; this, I suspect, fosters a tendency to conceptualise the two sides in warfare as members of opposing teams, each in their own uniform. No one volunteered this much to me, but the idea is lent support by the designs on the third Senglap set of co-ordinated shields, which are actually based on the Cambridge Cup, a national rugby league trophy for which teams such as Lae Brothers, Rabaul Muruks and Hagen Tigers compete annually (fig. 33). The point is reinforced by the inscription on the shield (left) shown in pl. 11, which explicitly represents the war between Dange and Senglap in team terms.

However, this team idiom appears to be restricted to shields used in North Wall fighting. I know of no sets of shields with coordinated 'team' designs from the fighting around Minj on the South Wall. This is not because rugby league as a sport is of any less significance there. Indeed, Bruce (1992:71) reports that the first major conflict of the 1989 warfare there between Konumbka and Kondika was actually sparked off by a rugby league match between two clan teams. Perhaps the non-adoption of coordinated shield designs on the part of Minj people is related to the fact that in one respect Minj warfare is becoming *less* team-like. Traditional fighting with shields involves a degree of cooperation amongst shield carriers, and between carriers and other warriors. Today, however, Minj people fear that home-made guns are being superseded by manufactured rifles whose bullets penetrate even metal shields, and

Fig. 33 Wooden shield; Senglap tribe, Olkanem subgroup. The 'Cambridge Cup' is a national rugby league competition; 1990 Oc.9.16; H: 165 cm.

one reason people there gave for their readiness to dispose of shields to me was that in future they would be fighting more individually, without the cooperative fighting strategy entailed by the use of shields.

On the North Wall, in contrast, Senglap men told me that they and their Dange opponents had agreed to forgo the use of guns, since too many people would otherwise be killed. Consequently, while each Senglap group was eager to sell a proportion of its shields, the possibility of the shields being needed in the future made them reluctant to dispose of more than a quota. So, while resorting to shields was in the past a sign of escalation in fighting, the use of shields today is also a reflection of the attempt to *contain* warfare.[10] Conceivably, this moderating aspect of contemporary shield use is also a clue to why it is apparently only groups on the North Wall, where fighting has been less lethal, which have drawn on the more playful world of sport for shield design. One or two of the North Wall shields also give the impression of being less substantial than their South Wall equivalents, though shields from both areas have their share of embedded arrow and spear tips.

If one of the coordinated sets of Senglap shields ('Six 2 Six') applied an idiom of sociability to the fighting, and the second ('Cambridge Cup') deployed a sporting metaphor, what are we to make of the final set, based on the advertisement for South Pacific beer? To put it theatrically, does this demonstrate that advertising has penetrated even into 'tribal warfare'? There is certainly no direct tie between Senglap Baiman, the subgroup which used the shields, and the South Pacific Brewery. This was not, as it were, sponsored warfare – the commercial equivalent of the sponsorship of masquerades in Sierra Leone by political parties there (Nunley 1987). On the other hand, without the existence of South Pacific beer and its advertisement, there would clearly have been no 'SP' shield design. Furthermore, this design was one which the artist, Kaipel Ka, had considerable proficiency at producing, since he regularly executed it in his work as a sign-painter.

If in these respects, shield design reflects the encroachment of commercial pressures, at another level the take-up and interpretation of those pressures is conditioned by local values.[11] Kaipel's own explanation of his use of the SP design was that he had been asked by senior men to incorporate a representation of a beer bottle on the shield, to make the point that 'it was beer alone which had precipitated this fighting'. (The war followed the breakdown of negotiations for compensation after an inebriated Senglap man had fallen from a Dange-owned vehicle.) Rather than including a picture of a beer bottle, Kaipel decided instead to make the point by using the SP design as a whole. At one level, then, this design parallels those that express regret. At another level, there is also something appropriate in the use of beer. Beer drinking is often a 'group' matter, just as warfare is. As Marie Reay (1982:164) observes 'Clansmen fight together; they also drink together'. It is perhaps not surprising, then, to find that the design for a product whose consumption has strong corporate associations in one sphere is being used to represent the group in another corporate activity, fighting.

In other respects, too, the designs used on these Senglap shields, while overtly externally derived, were reinterpreted locally. I was immediately struck, for example, by the presence of the two Raggiana birds of paradise perched on the skull in 'Six 2 Six' designs (pl. 13). The Raggiana bird of paradise has been made something of an emblem of the Papua New Guinean state, and a representation of the bird appears on the national crest, on currency and, incidentally, on the label for SP Export Lager. However, the bird also has a particular significance in the context of Wahgi warfare: 'Raggiana bird of paradise war' is the term for the most bitter type of conflict. The fact that a *pair* of birds, rather than the single one which appears elsewhere, was represented on the shields was also suggestive, since pairing is a characteristic Wahgi practice, and the groups who fight 'Raggiana bird of paradise war' are listed in pairs. The Senglap man whom I asked denied that these were the reasons behind the selection of this part of the design. However, it was interesting that one of my own Komblo friends immediately commented, upon seeing the shield, that the inclusion of the birds was a warning that the war between Senglap and Dange was in danger of escalating to 'Raggiana' proportions. In other words, motifs which are external in origin may be reinterpreted in local terms, even where this is not the reason for their selection in the first place.

Perhaps the complexity of this process of external influence and local appropriation is revealed most clearly in Kaipel's answer to my question as to why he often decorated shields with a border of red triangles (pl. 14). He explained that senior Senglap men had instructed him to incorporate a *geru* design (typically triangular) into the shield decoration. This was to allude to the fact that, following earlier warfare, Senglap and Dange had formerly been taboo to eating or drinking with each other (*geru*-wearing involves such taboos). The best way he thought he could do this, Kaipel told me, was to adapt to the purpose the rather similar triangular design associated with the packaging on the other well-known local beer, San Miguel (fig. 34). The result is a complex composite: a 'traditional' instruction to incorporate reference to the cause of a war through making one substitution ('*geru*' to stand for 'taboo') is creatively executed through another ('San Miguel design' for '*geru*').

Interesting parallels also emerged in the second category of artefacts I want to look at in detail: netbags.

Fig. 34 Design from San Miguel beer packaging, adopted as shield motif for its similarity to traditional *geru* designs. (After sketch by John Burton.)

Netbags

The technique of netting, or looping, is known in all the societies of the New Guinea hinterlands and Highlands. Its products include headnets, aprons, cloaks, arrow bindings and fishing nets, but undoubtedly its best known manifestation is the netbag. Like other netted items, netbags are looped from a single thread, spun on the thigh, to which new sections are continually added as work proceeds. Since the entire thread is pulled through the body of the work in the construction of each loop, the result is very strong, for a severed thread cannot unravel.

The use the Wahgi make of netbags fully justifies MacKenzie's (1991:2) description of these societies as netbag 'dependent'. Everything from harvested sweet potato to cartons of black-market beer is carried in the large, relatively loosely-netted work bags known as *kon mengel* (fig. 35). No less various are the uses of *kon kupn*, similarly-shaped decorative netbags into which soft marsupial fur has been spun. They are worn as items of adornment to attend a bridewealth payment or for a visit to the market; they may be exchanged

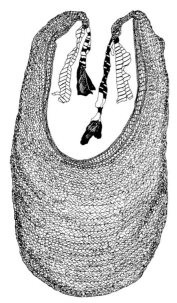

Fig. 35 *Kon mengel*: loosely-netted work netbag.

Fig. 36 Kangep's newborn is carried in the netbag on her back; its handles are cushioned against the work netbag bundled on her head. A third netbag is slung over her left shoulder and she is making a fourth. She has also draped a modern crocheted poncho over her shoulders (1990).

as informal gifts between women (until I began to collect netbags, I did not realise how widespread this latter practice was); later, they may serve as the cradle for a child (fig. 36). Netbags of this shape, whether 'work' or 'decorative', are most often worn by women and suspended from the forehead. *Kon kamban*, smaller, squarer bags, which may also be slung over the shoulder or round the neck, are used by both sexes to carry personal possessions. Yet other kinds of bags, worn by men under the arm, serve as portable caches for war- or love-magic (fig. 37). In the past, netbags were also used in a kind of externalised autopsy: a dead man's wealth might be wrapped in new bark-cloth and stored overnight in a netbag; the following morning the bundle would be unwrapped and inspected for small specks which were taken as clues to the cause of death. Old netbags also formerly served as widow's weeds: a man's ghost was felt to inhere in the heavy mass of netbags which was draped over his widow's head.

As an artefact with such a wide range of uses, the netbag has also traditionally been a rich source of local metaphor. Though not all Wahgi women make netbags, and not all netbags are made by women (again, it was making the collection which drew my attention to the existence of the exceptions), netbags are associated with women rather than with men in Wahgi society. The marriage rule referred to in the last chapter, whereby a set of brothers should offer a girl in marriage back to their mother's clan, translates literally as 'giving a skull in a netbag', and 'netbag' may also be used as a synonym for both bride and womb. The way in which a netbag is worn also denotes ideas of female attractiveness: eligible girls are said to wear their netbags *gop ol*: knotted so the handles are long and the bag extends well down the back.

As MacKenzie (1991:2) has sketched for New Guinea as a whole, netbags have not succumbed to imported alternatives. In certain respects they have even extended their role, incorporating new materials and designs, enlarging their scope as metaphors and expanding into regions of New Guinea where hitherto they had not been made. Here I take the example of Wahgi netbags to put some local flesh on the complex process of transformation and continuity to which MacKenzie's study has pointed for New Guinea more generally.

While some Wahgi work-netbags do continue to be looped from traditional fibres, many are now made from such introduced materials as extruded nylon or from unravelled and re-spun rice bags, or unpicked garments.[12] These new materials have some technical advantages (for example, sweet potato can be washed in artificial fibre netbags without the bag rotting) but also drawbacks (such netbags may begin to melt if left very close to a fire). Decorative netbags, whether of the *kupn* or *kamban* types, are now very largely made from highly-saturated acrylic yarns (pl. 15). This has not, however, meant the abandonment of marsupial fur, which continues to be spun into such bags.

Along with the adoption of the new materials has come the opportunity to work them into fresh designs. Initially, Wahgi women made rather restrained use of the new acrylic yarns which they purchased with their coffee income. In the 1970s most *kupn* netbags, for example, were simply made in alternating blue and white, or black and white stripes. In the following decade, however, women began to produce such bags in the multi-coloured stripes which they see as characteristic of those made by Mt. Hagen women, whose taste they admire.

Acrylic yarns have had an even more striking impact on the smaller *kamban* netbags. The names for the designs netted into these latter bags capture something of the changing experience of Highlanders. Some designs, such as 'Cross' (fig. 38) and perhaps 'Christmas' (fig. 39; also known as 'Forestry') are clearly influenced by the missionary presence; others, such as 'One Ace' (fig. 40), and possibly 'Diamond', reflect the popularity of playing cards. Another – 'Yonki Pawa' – derives from technological change, Yonki (map 1) being the site of a major new power-generating station in the Eastern Highlands, whose pylons are modelled in this netbag's design (fig. 41). At least one name – 'Mandang' (fig. 42) – adverts to the supposed origin place of the style (the province or town of Madang). 'Skin Pik' (fig. 43) suggests the roadside markets at which many of these new designs are worn (it is named after its resemblance to the lattice of squares into which pork is divided for sale at markets). Other designs include 'Snake', 'Walkabout' and 'Mountain'.

These designs are not local to the Wahgi; instead, women regard them as being imported, often from specific directions, rather in the same way that different kinds of shell used to travel 'from up-river down' or vice versa. 'One Ace', for example, like the practice of making multi-coloured *kupn* bags, is

Fig. 37 Love-magic bag; amongst its decorations are rip-tops from beer bottles, marsupial jawbones and sea shells. 1986 Oc.4.49; w: 23 cm.

Fig. 38 'Cross' design.

Fig. 39 'Christmas' or 'Forestry' design.

Fig. 40 'One Ace' design.

said to have arrived quite recently from Hagen to the west. 'Yonki Pawa' and 'Mountain', in contrast, are said to be new designs just now reaching the Wahgi area from Simbu and Goroka to the east. Pangia in the Southern Highlands, though never on a direct shell-route, is seen as the source of the equally recent practice of making *kupn* bags in a single colour (often black or white), with a few very thin horizontal lines in vividly contrasting hues.

The shape and size of netbags are also indicative of their area of origin, though these two elements do not appear to be mobile in the way that designs are. Wahgi women show little sign of wishing to emulate what they see as the enormous size of some Enga netbags, or to produce *kupn* bags with the short handles, shallow belly and dense marsupial fur characteristic of Simbu. To the extent that their design, shape and size are indeed associated with different parts of New Guinea, netbags now have the additional capacity to act as markers of local identity in the 'self-conscious regionalist displays' which, MacKenzie (1991:14) notes, now take place in towns like Port Moresby.

Wahgi women acquire these new designs in different ways. Sometimes, they say, it is simply through spotting one, perhaps on a visit to town, and deducing how it must be made. Other designs are explicitly taught by immigrants from the area in question, either in-married wives or the spouses of labour migrants working on Wahgi coffee plantations. Mai, Magistrate Dop's Hagen wife, for example, taught a number of Komblo women how to make 'One Ace', though Gulka, Kaunga's wife, also claims that she introduced the style to Komblo, after she had been taught it by a Hagen fellow-patient in Kudjip Hospital. The two Pangia-style bags I purchased were made respectively by a Pangia women married into Kulaka and, slightly less expertly, by a Wahgi woman herself natally of Kulaka. Wahgi coffee wealth thus pulls in not merely wives from other areas but new netbag designs along with them.

Netbags have simultaneously become an idiom in terms of which to debate the future of Wahgi cultural practices and male and female roles. This often emerges with regard to how netbags are worn, different verbs being used according to whether a netbag is suspended from the forehead (*menge*) or slung over the shoulder (*tamne*). It was in these terms, for example, that one man denied that Komblo would ever hold another Pig Festival. Women today, he claimed, were no longer capable of supporting from their foreheads the great netbags of sweet potato necessary to feed Festival pigs. Instead, they simply idled around wearing small decorative *kamban* netbags over their shoulders.[13] Not everyone agreed – one friend commenting that the remark was true only of the man's own wife, noted as an inveterate gambler.

However, the concern that young women today are idling around, rather than working in their appointed roles, is reflected in another frequent comment: that a woman who wears her netbag other than suspended from the forehead is 'loose' (*na-mengnem, pasingia amb*). Josephine Goi made even finer distinctions, according to the particular *way* a netbag was worn over the shoulder: to wear it like a bandoleer was the sign of a woman 'who wanted to take over her husband's role', to wear a bag suspended round the neck like a bib was the mark of a prostitute. The significance attributed to the way in which netbags are worn also emerged in one middle-aged couple's reflections on the kind of wife they wanted for their son. They favoured, they said, someone from one of the remoter Wahgi tribes such as Monglka, a girl who had been brought up to work hard, not someone with fancy ways from the main Wahgi Valley, always throwing a netbag over her shoulder and going off to the market.

Finally, it is interesting briefly to compare the new netbag designs with those on shields. Lettering, though much rarer than on shield designs, is occasionally incorporated into contemporary Wahgi netbags. In one instance, this involved the inclusion of people's names (fig. 44). The names in question, however, were not those of the maker or carrier (as would have been the case on a shield), but of the maker's Sepik husband and daughter. The only other instance I saw was on a bag made for sale to tourists, and which carried a representation of the Papua New Guinean flag, with the words 'PNG Beautiful Country' on the reverse (see back cover). There were no netbag designs based on commodities, whether on brands of beer or on other products which might be thought to have more 'female' connotations. Nor were wives on the same 'path' – that is, married in from the same other clan – said to have similar netbag designs (though such wives *are* meant to wear the same type of special cordyline bustle when bridewealth is handed over). And predictably, perhaps, the clan context of much shield design was also largely absent: there were no dates or taunts inscribed into netbags, or sets of netbags co-ordinated around sporting trophies like the 'Cambridge Cup' shield design. The only indication of an intriguing exception lay in Josephine Goi's remark that some women now incorporated the colours of their husbands' or boyfriends' rugby league clubs into their netbags.

As the collection increased in size, so my field base became crowded. Artefacts were tucked into the cane walls, propped against house posts, and suspended from the rafters; the place itself came to resemble a museum. Their presence stimulated visitors to perform mini-dramas, demonstrating how this or that object would formerly have been employed. Waiang, a senior woman in the settlement, was inspired to don the charcoal and netbags formerly worn by widows (fig. 45). A strand from a skirt was attached to a particularly fine pearl shell to illustrate how such a valuable would have been offered as an inducement to kill an enemy.

The shields, in particular, exercised a magnetic pull over Komblo men, few of whom could resist giving energetic demonstrations of their use: a reflection, perhaps, of the specific history of such middle-aged men, who had lived childhoods dominated by warfare and refugeeship but who have not themselves had to carry shields in battle. If this was their fetish, my own anticipated the shields' future as museum artefacts, and I worried that these vigorous demonstrations of their use would damage the paintwork of the shield designs. Eventually Kinden tired of my fussing, telling me that while I might know about *buk konngan* ('book work'), the robustness of Wahgi artefacts was something in which *he* was the expert.

The way in which people react to the making of a collection tells us, in fact, something about their historical experience. In such areas as the Southern Highlands, which were subjected to colonial pressure that was even more sudden and overwhelming than was the case in the Western Highlands, making a collection may precipitate an emotional rediscovery of what was lost or suppressed in local culture (Stürzenhofecker, personal communication,

Fig. 41 'Yonki Pawa' design.

Fig. 42 'Mandang' design.

Fig. 43 'Skin Pik' design.

Fig. 44 Netbag incorporating the names of the maker's daughter and husband as part of its design. 1990 Oc.9.74; w: 46 cm.

from fieldwork amongst the Duna people of Lake Kopiago).

The Wahgi instance was rather different. Certain items, such as the *bolyim* house which I thought I might commission, most men were simply not prepared to make. Equally, after reflection, people abandoned their initial enthusiasm for staging a mock battle to mark my first departure from the field. Both *bolyim* houses and warfare remain sufficiently integral to on-going culture for it to be dangerous to invoke them without due cause. But the many cultural practices which *were* re-enacted in the context of making the collection did not seem to me to be done in any mood of emotional rediscovery. Rather, demonstrations of how stone axes used to be made, or of how highly pearl shells were formerly valued, tended to be carried out with a caricatured seriousness which collapsed into laughter. There was sometimes a sense that people felt they had been absurd to esteem shells in the way they had, to have laboured as long as they did to grind hard stones down to make axes. Now they knew better.[14] Making items for the collection and demonstrating their use was, for the Wahgi, less a rediscovery of culture from which they had been estranged than a marker of how far they had come. Indeed, it was in the context of my collecting that some younger people encountered such items as wooden pandanus bowls and *geru* boards for the first time: such artefacts were becoming museum pieces in a double sense.

The notion that such older material cultural forms are becoming 'museumified' is supported by the recent establishment of the remarkable Onga Cultural Centre at Romonga, just to the west of the Wahgi culture area (Burton 1991). There are a number of other museums and cultural centres in the Highlands. Most, however, are officially-established and -funded institutions (though in the case of one of them, described by Frankel [1986:30-2], the institution was interpreted by the local Huli people as a forum in which the relative truth of indigenous and introduced religions could finally be settled, and action taken to arrest the world's slide into entropy). The Onga Cultural Centre, in contrast, appears to be entirely a local initiative. It was established in the late 1980s by Yap Kupal, a Romonga man of about forty, and comprises a traditional Hagen man's house and a woman's house from the pre-contact period, re-created with what seemed to me exceptional fidelity and stocked with a truly remarkable array of material culture. Yap (fig. 46), who emphasised to me that he was uneducated, said that he had wanted to make such a museum after seeing the ones in Port Moresby and elsewhere. His main motive for doing so was precisely so that in the future people should know how their forefathers had lived; to get the details right he had gone round interrogating older people.

I was only able to spend half a morning there but the Onga Cultural Centre seemed to have very much the atmosphere that traditional Western museums are conventionally supposed to possess: slightly musty, a place apart from normal social life. It did not appear to function as a community meeting house or men's house, the kind of indigenous institution which such writers as Mead (1983) have suggested is the appropriate model for museums in the Third World. Some of Yap's objects even had labels attached. The labels, however, gave the prices of the artefacts: not, according to Yap, the amount he might be prepared to sell each object for, but rather what he had himself paid for them. (Yap's displays thus anticipated the point made by the curators of a

Fig. 45 Making the collection prompted Wahgi to demonstrate discontinued cultural practices. Here Waiang dresses in the chains of cane loops, charcoal and netbags formerly worn by widows; left, Lina (1990).

radical exhibition held recently in Oxford, that museum labels should include prices in order to expose the market forces behind museums and the artefacts they acquire [Beard and Henderson, 1991]). But it was also interesting that in other respects, Yap's focus is entirely upon traditional material culture, narrowly conceived. He did not, for example, display the ribbing from a sock alongside a traditional woven legband as an illustration that the two were at one level 'the same'. All this suggests that despite the many underlying cultural continuities to which I have drawn attention, at another level people do also perceive considerable discontinuity.

Though Yap emphasised that his cultural centre was largely to preserve the past for the future, it was also intended as a tourist attraction. The potential marketability of Wahgi culture had also been a theme a decade earlier during the Pig Festival, when Yimbal (see Chapter 1) and his brothers had spoken to me about the possibility of establishing a village in which Komblo could perform a range of traditional activities for the benefit of paying tourists (a

Fig. 46 Yap Kupal (holding stone axes made for sale to tourists) is the founder of an indigenous museum; left, Kekanem Kinden (1990).

Fig. 47 The crates in which the collection travelled were labelled by Kaipel, the shield painter; Yimbal Aipe (subsequently elected as MP for the North Wahgi) at the wheel (1990).

Fig. 48 Wheeled toy, decorated by the maker with the museum's initials as observed on the crates, and with the South Pacific beer slogan. 1990 Oc.9.615; L: 230 cm.

local version, in fact, of the performances which Cultural Cooperation were later to bring to Europe). This was also one of the reasons for which I was praised for having written an earlier book describing Wahgi adornment (O'Hanlon 1989). The merit of the book, I was told, was that in future other groups who copied Wahgi cultural practice to make money from tourists could be asked to pay copyright. All this suggests that culture is becoming commoditised, seen as 'heritage' that can be marketed. If at one level this is so, at another, it is of course not entirely without traditional parallel. As I noted in the previous chapter, most of the components of the Pig Festival, including the *bolyim* house itself, have over the years been moving westward, sold on by one group to another.

As my period in the Highlands drew to a close, I felt a growing sense of interpenetration between Wahgi frames of reference and my collecting. I overheard Kinden, who had accompanied me to Yap Kupal's Cultural Centre, suggesting that, once I left, a museum should be set up at Topkalap. The crates (fig. 47) which Michael Du had made for the collection had to be painted with the Museum of Mankind's address, and labelled as 'fragile'. It was important that this should be done legibly to minimise the risk of damage, or of the crates going astray. The only practised painter I knew was Kaipel, who had decorated many of the shields which the crates now contained, and he spent an afternoon meticulously labelling them. Pilo then used the abbreviated version of the museum's name ('MoM'), which he saw on the crates, in a decorative dedication on the elaborate *wilwil* toy he was constructing for the collection (fig. 48).

Similar complexities, and the extent to which my collecting activities had been partly assimilated to local frames of reference, emerged when the first of the collections I made in the Wahgi was being packed. On the one hand, the collection was a project which, in being exported, would be launched on a wider stage. It would 'be revealed', as Wahgi say of items like *geru* boards and ceremonial wigs. Before such objects are publicly revealed, those launching them solicit ghostly support through consuming a private sacrificial meal. As he outlined the arrangements for the meal he organised for the collection's departure, Kinden commented that he did not know who *my* ancestors were: the unspoken implication was that it would be *his* ancestors whose ghostly help would be sought.

On the other hand, the completion of the collection was also a leave-taking. If there is a single model for leave-taking in Wahgi society it is that of marriage, when a girl departs her natal kin to live among her husband's clanspeople. There were now indications that this model was being applied to the departure of the collection. Anamb, the local ritual expert, and a long-time friend but also someone who, on occasion, felt himself challenged by Kinden's sponsorship of me, proposed that the collection should undergo the ceremony of beautification which is performed for a bride the evening before her departure. This was a suggestion with considerable political spin on it, a point I also noted when the same idiom of kinship was invoked in negotiating what was to be paid for artefacts. For if the collection was like a bride, then what I had paid for it was like bridewealth; and the point about bridewealth is that it is only the *first* of the payments which are owed to a bride's kin. A bride's brothers also expect payments for the children which subsequently flow from her, for they are the children's 'source people'. Anamb's comparison was his way of highlighting my continuing relationship of indebtedness to those who had helped me, as well as a specific attempt to constitute himself as the 'source person' of any benefit which might flow to me from the collection.

CHAPTER THREE

Exhibiting in Practice

T here are a number of reasons for concluding this book with a sketch of the circumstances of staging the exhibition which it accompanies. The chief one is to spell out for the process of 'exhibiting' the point made about 'collecting' in the previous chapter: that neither process happens in a vacuum. Both activities, rather, take place in a given context and that context (particular fieldwork situation on the one hand, specific museum on the other) inevitably influences the image of a culture which an exhibition portrays.

There has, in fact, been a flood of such reflexive writing on museums and exhibitions since Clifford (1988:229) argued that 'it is important to resist the tendency of collections to be self-sufficient, to suppress their own historical, economic, and political processes of production . . . Ideally, the history of its own collection and display should be a visible aspect of any exhibition'.[1] To date, however, these discussions have tended to focus more exclusively upon theoretical issues – on, for example, the nature and politics of representation – than upon the mechanics of the production of specific exhibitions which, like the Wahgi *bolyim* house, tend to be prepared out of sight and revealed only when the processes which went into the making of them have been concealed.[2] While such issues as representation are touched upon in what follows, I try to provide more information than is generally done on the chronology, constraints and practical aspects of mounting a specific exhibition in changing circumstances. I outline the reasons for holding the exhibition, sketch the location and galleries in which it will be held, and give the thinking behind its intended layout.

The dearth of such information is highlighted by the way that ethnographic exhibitions are sometimes reviewed. Let me take as a minor example one aspect of the review of an exhibition, held in fact at the Museum of Mankind in 1987, which included material on the religious practices of Bolivian mining communities. I take this example because it illustrates the more widespread failure of museums to convey, and of reviewers to visualise, the context in which exhibitions actually happen. Criticising the exhibition's use of a glass-case format for most of the objects on display, the reviewer (Platt 1987:13-14) remarks:

> What a missed opportunity! We could have entered a cavernous tunnel, stumbling on tracks driving into the darkness, caught a glimpse of ore-laden trucks, a cage and a mineshaft, of the *barretero* [pickman] at the rock face, and then – incredulously – of a wicked-looking goblin amidst the

block-cavings before arriving at the seated effigies . . . An exhibition plunged in near-darkness, carefully lit, and with adjoining 'windows' on specific topics and collateral activities in Oruro City and the countryside outside . . . Visitors could even have been offered miners' helmets and lamps on entry . . .

The assumption here is that an exhibition should be like a film-set, reconstructing as vividly as possible the artefacts' original context – an issue to which I return below. This assumption aside, it is not necessarily lack of vision so much as mundane contextual factors of cost and practicality which cause such opportunities to be 'missed'. Both the gallery in question and the exhibition budget were a fraction of the size necessary for so elaborate a treatment. Such factors – along with issues of safety and security (in the advocated 'near-darkness') and staffing levels (necessary to dispense, re-claim and repair miners' helmets) – exert an unseen influence on the form taken by exhibitions. Like other enterprises, exhibitions cannot adequately be assessed without reference to the particular context in which they take place.[3]

This chapter, then, is written for visitors and for others interested in knowing something of how a particular exhibition comes to look as it does; for visiting any exhibition does potentially raise questions at two distinct levels. On the one hand, it may pose questions about the individual objects included in it; on the other, about the exhibition as an entity in its own right: why are some objects included but not others; why are they grouped in this way, and not that; why is one subject tackled but another ignored? In earlier sections I have described the repeated interpenetration of field and museum contexts: how the Hagen dancers' European tour created expectations as to why I was re-visiting the Wahgi, how local group structure affected the order in

Fig. 50 Wooden shield, Senglap tribe. The parallel slanting bands show its original colour, grime free. 1990 Oc.9.8; H: 158 cm.

OPPOSITE
Plate 9 At the conclusion of the Festival, pigs are clubbed around the *bolyim* house, *mond* post and cross; *geru* boards have been placed on a number of the pigs. (1980)

which objects were acquired for the collection, how my collecting activities stimulated talk of founding a museum in the Wahgi, and how the Museum of Mankind's initials were inscribed on new artefacts which were then offered for sale. In this final chapter, I also sustain this theme by paying to the fabrication of the exhibition a measure of the same attention as was earlier given to Wahgi shields and netbags.

However, much though one is needed, this chapter cannot be a full account of staging an exhibition. Bouquet (1991:163) remarks that 'The inner ethnographies of museums, their collections and the human relations between permanent staff and those who are drawn into their fields of influence in one way and another, have yet to be written. When they are, they may prove more delicate and explosive than the recently detonated ethnographies which have caused such stirrings on both sides of the Atlantic.' It is not, however, for reasons of explosivity that this account is incomplete – though prudence is likely to mean that ethnographies of institutions as fraught as those to which Bouquet alludes are unlikely to be written by insiders.

The omissions I have in mind are, rather, those dictated first by the limited space available in this chapter and second by publishing schedules. Artefacts added to the museum's collection – whether they come directly from the field or elsewhere – are channelled through processes of fumigation, registration, labelling, conservation, photography and storage. Within the confines of a short chapter I cannot describe all these – though beneath their apparently self-explanatory, technical nature they necessarily embody cultural choices. Van Beek (1990), indeed, has questioned the popular metaphor which portrays museums as mausoleums, and their storage areas as 'object cemeteries', symptomatic of an arid, peculiarly Western approach to objects. He argues (1990:33), rather, that the period any object spends in storage is not a neutral passage of time but becomes instead a 'distinct attribute of the object itself'. This is so whether the object is cached in a New Guinea Men's House or in a museum's repository, and whether it is periodically retrieved from storage for a local ceremony or for a museum exhibition. Rather than the fundamentally artificial institutions they are so often portrayed as being, museums are simply 'the institutionalization and professionalization of a layered, fragmented and discontinuous view of objects that is itself a common cultural practice'.[4]

Equally, if this cycle of storage and use in a sense creates objective time (as the intervals between exhibition), so the process of museum conservation offers to arrest time. I was struck, for example, by the questions which the museum's conservation staff asked as they worked on the Wahgi artefacts. One of the shields (fig. 50) had been stored in a smoky house roof, only partially protected by a plastic wrapping: should the accumulated grime be removed from the shield's outer surface? The question raised the issue of what it is that an artefact is valued as embodying. Is it the shield as a perfect example of its type, a kind of snapshot in time, taken grime-free at the outset of its career? Or do we seek, rather, to preserve the evidence of the shield's biography through time, even when (as with the grime) the evidence also begins to obscure something of the artefact's original purpose?

Similar dilemmas had earlier arisen in the Wahgi with regard to Kunump's shield, shown in pl. 11. The paintwork of the design was peeling badly at

Plate 10 'Becoming one': representatives from Komblo and their former enemies snap a spear to mark the formal end to the hostilities which had separated them half a century earlier. (1980)

Plate 11 Contemporary Wahgi shields. As home-made guns entered inter-group fighting during the later 1980s, some men abandoned wooden shields (LEFT) in favour of metal ones (RIGHT). The shield on the left draws on the imagery of rugby league to portray the opposing sides as two teams: 'Danga Muruks' and 'Karapka [an antique term for Senglap tribe] SP Brothers'; the shield's background decoration is based on an advertisement for South Pacific lager ('No. 1 beer'). The legend on the shield on the right ('Kunump Superman') refers to the owner's size and forcefulness ('Bulldozer').

Plate 12 Local buses facilitate marriage and other links between the Wahgi and the rest of the Highlands; 'Six to Six' is the term for a 6pm to 6am party. (1990)

Plate 13 The renewal of inter-group fighting in the 1980s saw some groups coordinate their shield designs; here 'Six 2 Six' refers to Senglap Gilgalkup's claim to be able to fight from 6am to 6pm. (1990)

Plate 15 Contemporary netbags, made from acrylic yarns into which marsupial fur has been spun, worn by spectators at a marriage ceremony. (1990)

Plate 14 Kaipel Ka sometimes fought alongside his maternal kin and so decorated his own shield with the South Pacific beer logo otherwise used on theirs. (1990)

the time I purchased it. Learning that the design had been produced by Kaipel the sign-writer, I commissioned him to restore it to its original condition. Whether this is a loss or gain in authenticity depends upon perspective. The re-painting certainly erased from the shield some of the testimony of its age and use; on the other hand, it also restored evidence, in the form of the original design, much of which had flaked off. A further complication ensued from Kaipel's assumption that, while I might want him to re-paint his design, the museum would hardly be interested in the lettering towards the base advertising his sign-writing business; this he omitted. On examining the re-painted shield, I noticed the absence and asked him to include the lettering. At one level, this completed the restoration of the shield's original appearance, but at the cost of erasing evidence of Kaipel's own understanding of what might be appropriate on a museum artefact.[5]

Publishing deadlines similarly dictate that much of the ethnography of the exhibition's design and mounting is also omitted, since these will take place only after this manuscript must go to press. This chapter, then, necessarily represents work in progress, and reflects, moreover, only one of the many contributions which go to make up an exhibition. Yet this unavoidable incompleteness has an illustrative aspect. A frequent tactic in exhibitions is to include examples of the earlier stages of manufacture of a given artefact, with the idea of showing how the finished object comes to look as it does. To the extent that this account is incomplete, it stands in a similar relation to the exhibition in its final form.

Before going on to discuss the location of the exhibition and its intended layout at the time of writing, it is worth reviewing the reasons for mounting an exhibition on this subject in the first place. First, it presented an opportunity to exhibit the Wahgi material that was in the process of being acquired for the museum – further tangible results of the Trustees' emphasis on adding to the museum's holdings through making documented field collections rather than relying on auction-house purchases.

A second point in favour of a Wahgi exhibition was the almost complete absence elsewhere in the world of exhibitions focusing on the New Guinea Highlands.[6] From one point of view this absence is odd. Since their 'discovery' in the 1930s, the peoples of the New Guinea Highlands have been among the most intensively studied on the globe, and data from the area has been at the forefront of anthropological debates for the past thirty years. At another level, however, the dearth of exhibitions undoubtedly reflects most museums' orientation to artefacts which are more permanent and 'collectable' than is much New Guinea Highlands material culture. On occasion, this museum perspective can feed back to influence indigenous communities' self-perception. Cruikshank (1992:8) describes how one Native American student from the interior of British Columbia reasoned that because her people did not have such sculptural forms as the totem poles produced by coastal peoples, they therefore lacked culture itself. In fact, many of the changes in Wahgi society documented in the previous chapters (whether the boosted imports of shells, or the incorporation of such new materials as acrylic yarns and paints) have conspired to make Wahgi culture more 'exhibitable' than formerly.

A further merit of such an exhibition was the opportunity it provided for

OPPOSITE
Plate 16 Kala Wala, decorated for the presentation of her bridewealth. The Papua New Guinean currency in her armbands is a gift from her natal clanspeople, and she wears the rip-tops from beer bottles as earrings. (1980)

the museum's education programme to question the stereotype (reflected in many of the enquiries which ethnography museums receive) that countries such as Papua New Guinea remain largely untouched by the contemporary industrialised world. *Living Arctic*, an earlier Museum of Mankind exhibition, had sought to undermine the same stereotype for the indigenous peoples of northern Canada, and visitors regularly recorded their surprise in the 'comments' book kept in the exhibition at 'how up-to-date' 'they' were. There is, though, a particular need to do this in relation to Papua New Guinea, whose popular image in the West tends to be exclusively that of the last refuge of exotic practices – a point illustrated by the television report on the visiting Hagen dancers. The inclusion in the exhibition of the full range of manufactured goods used by the Wahgi should challenge this admittedly evergreen stereotype. Accompanying photographs and text will make the equally important complementary point that the incorporation of Western goods does not determine how they are used and is not the simple index of acculturation it is sometimes taken to be.

Site and 'set'

Having placed the artefacts in their Wahgi Valley setting in Chapter 1, I want briefly to sketch their location while on exhibition. Number 6 Burlington Gardens, the building presently occupied by the British Museum's Ethnogra-

Fig. 51 London University's new building in 1870; a century later, the building became the Museum of Mankind.

phy Department, was not purpose-built as a museum. Designed in the 1860s by James Pennethorne (adopted son of the architect John Nash), its first tenants were London University, hence the statues along the façade of luminaries ranging from Plato to Adam Smith (fig. 51). Subsequently, the building housed the Civil Service Commission, before hosting the Ethnography Department when it migrated from the British Museum's overcrowded Bloomsbury site in 1970.

A number of the building's grand rooms are occupied by relatively permanent displays; others are devoted to equally long term functions such as a Film Theatre, a Library and Schools' and Students' Rooms. Broadly, this leaves three double galleries, each some 550 square metres in area, in which to stage 'temporary' exhibitions. The comparatively short life span of these exhibitions (recently averaging some two years) recognises that much ethnographic material is insufficiently robust to be exposed for longer periods; over time, it also allows more of the stored collections to be displayed than would 'permanent' exhibitions in the same space. Most temporary exhibitions erected in these three galleries have also differed from the more permanent exhibitions in terms of display technique. Rather than simply grouping artefacts by type or culture, or with a view to highlighting their aesthetic qualities, many of these temporary exhibitions have sought to recreate something of the artefacts' original physical surroundings. External contractors, supervised by the museum's Design Office and assisted by museum technical staff, have

Fig. 52 Planned adaptation of pre-existing exhibition 'set'.

▨	Platform
▦	Wall
▦	Structural pier
☐	Wallcase

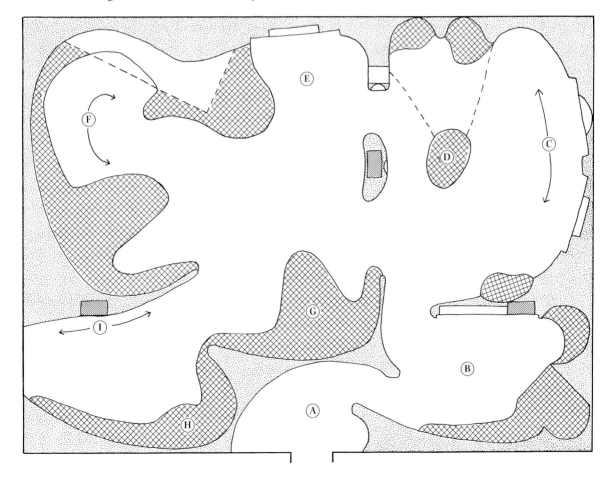

simulated tropical forests, Arctic landscapes, Malagasy and Indian villages and a Yemeni market.

It was in this context that, in the late 1980s, I proposed a large exhibition on the Wahgi to go into one of the three double galleries. The exhibition was scheduled to follow one entitled *Palestinian Costume*, to which Palestinian and other Arab sponsors had made substantial financial contributions. Their assistance had allowed the double gallery in which the exhibition was held to be fitted out with an attractive 'set' (fig. 52). Curved false walls, intended to suggest the hills and open spaces of Palestine, were erected within the gallery as a backdrop to the costumes, which were displayed on raised platforms. My own exhibition brief anticipated using the rooms of this double gallery (once they had been stripped of the Palestinian set) to represent two kinds of time. The first room would model historical time, carrying visitors from the stone artefacts of the first gardeners of the Wahgi Valley, through the kaleidoscope of changes outlined in Chapter 1, to the present. The second room would be devoted to the ritual time of the Pig Festival, with visitors moving around a circular walk taking them through the material culture of the Festival cycle. Looking towards the centre of the room, they would see the *bolyim* house and *mond* post in their various stages; looking outward, they would see the artefacts associated with the different moments of the Festival. As initially conceived, then, the exhibition would have made extensive use of reconstruction – rather as advocated by the reviewer of the Bolivian exhibition.

Meanwhile, however, the broader context for holding such an exhibition was itself moving. Large exhibitions of this kind are not cheap to produce professionally. Precise costs depend upon the degree of elaboration of the exhibition but often run to several hundred pounds per square metre of exhibition space. Museums are also highly labour-intensive institutions in which staff salaries absorb the major proportion of their running costs. In common with many other publicly-funded bodies over the course of the 1980s, financial provision for museums has not kept pace with staff costs (Wilson 1989:95). Increasingly, elaborate exhibitions of the kind I had proposed require supplementary sponsorship. While efforts to attract funds continue as this is written, to date no major sponsorship for a New Guinea Highlands exhibition has been obtained. Indeed, if sponsorship becomes a necessary condition for putting on elaborate exhibitions, it must inevitably influence which topics and cultures are displayed in this way.

The answer, as I write, is to scale the exhibition down to a single gallery, and to stage it within the framework given by the Palestinian 'set', which would be inordinately costly to dismantle and replace, given the planned return of the Ethnography Department to the main British Museum site in Bloomsbury in the next few years. Although designed to evoke the Palestinian landscape, the existing set is otherwise relatively neutral in character, and the raised platforms on which costumes were exhibited can equally be used to display Wahgi material. The pattern of islands and platforms does, of course, impose something of a pre-set format on the shape that the exhibition can take. It is not altogether inappropriate, though, that an exhibition, one of whose themes is re-contextualisation, should itself be staged within a space designed with a rather different effect in mind. Moreover, all exhibitions happen within limits, and these particular ones do at least dispense at the outset with the illusion of complete naturalness which not even the most faithful reconstruction can sustain indefinitely.

In the period since initially conceiving the exhibition the use of naively naturalistic reconstructions has, in fact, increasingly come to be questioned. Reconstructions were introduced into many ethnographic museums from the late 1960s as a more imaginative and less alienating alternative to displaying artefacts in glass cases: the Museum of Mankind, as it happens, was a pioneer in this respect. However, innovations in their turn inevitably become the starting point for fresh departures. While reconstructed environments and mannequins remain popular with many, to others they have come to seem doubly inauthentic. Not only are they not 'the real thing', but in so dramatically supplying artefacts with their 'original' context they tend to exclude the other contexts in which the artefacts have figured, including their present one as museum objects (Durrans 1988:162). This limitation to reconstruction as a technique brings to mind Baxandall's (1991:41) comment that 'exhibitors cannot *represent* cultures': all they can do, he suggests, is to set up a non-misleading and stimulating arena in which the maker of artefacts, the exhibitor's intentions and the visitor all come together. Such a perspective does not exclude the use of reconstructions. It simply suggests that their use should be undercut by some acknowledgement of their artificial status: at the end of this account I propose one way in which this might be done.

What follows, then, is a brief sketch of how, some eight months before the exhibition is due to open, I anticipate that the pre-existing layout shown in fig. 52 might be adapted for the purposes of the exhibition. Since this plan has yet to be scrutinised in detail by the exhibition designer there may be some divergence between the sketch and the exhibition as eventually realised. However, any divergence should affect neither the artefacts to be displayed nor the rationale for including them; merely the order in which they are exhibited. Differences are unlikely to be great, since, atypically, the existing 'set' is largely a given.[7] Any differences that do arise will also mean that this text remains as evidence of the provisionality which (as all those involved know) is inherent in exhibition-making.

In addition to the constraints imposed by the pre-existing Palestinian 'set', one further defining limit should be mentioned at the outset. This is simply the stock of artefacts available for inclusion in the exhibition. The Wahgi field collection numbers some 900 items in total. It is particularly strong in netbags, shields and shell ornaments but also includes examples of most of the artefact categories described in the course of the first two chapters, with the exception of bird of paradise plume headdresses, whose export is prohibited. Though financial constraints did not allow this deficiency to be made good through museum loans from abroad, I have been able to draw upon an extensive photographic collection to illustrate their use. I have also been given access to the unique archive of photographs taken by Mick Leahy. There are in addition a certain number of artefacts collected by Leahy and Taylor in British institutions, though none within the British Museum's own collections.

Exhibition Outline

The gallery in which the exhibition is to take place lies at the end of a corridor. A striking image, and title, is needed on the far wall of the antechamber (**A** in fig. 52) to draw visitors down this passage. As an exhibition title, *Paradise* is intentionally equivocal. Although the exhibition certainly concerns the Pacific, and the magnificence of the Wahgi Valley immediately impressed itself upon Leahy and Taylor, as it has on all visitors since, the 'paradise' alluded to is not the cliché of a palm-fringed South Seas beach. The title partly refers, of course, to the birds of paradise, whose plumes have had such a significant role in the decorative repertoire, status system and economy of the Wahgi and neighbouring peoples. But 'Paradise' also alludes to the range of material goods which coffee income has brought to the area over the last two decades, and which feature in the exhibition. A number of these goods themselves use 'Paradise' as a brand name – South Pacific lager, for example, advertises itself as 'the Beer of Paradise', and there are 'Paradise' biscuits for sale in trade-stores. Finally, if more remotely, the title also suggests the alternative paths to salvation offered by the many missions which now compete for Highlanders' support.

Whatever photographic image was selected to accompany the title had to be contemporary. To use one of the black and white Leahy images, striking as some are, would risk suggesting that the Wahgi came into being only with their 'discovery', and that they belonged essentially to the past (an impression which I also sought to avoid in Chapter 1 by 'placing' the Wahgi in the Valley, before 'discovering' them through an account of the Leahy-Taylor expedition). The photograph which it is planned to use instead is the portrait on the cover of this book, showing Kulka Kokn during the Komblo Pig Festival. With his headdress of red, yellow and black plumes, golden wig, and painted face, he presents an extravagantly 'traditional' image. Yet the face-paint he wears is commercially produced, not made from the pre-contact ochres; the mass adoption of black plumes by the Wahgi is a relatively recent phenomenon, partly reflecting Wahgi coffee wealth; and the bamboo frame of the wig is covered with imported fabric. As such, the photograph condenses the two themes of Wahgi interaction with the wider world, and the use of exogenous materials to re-work local culture, which are developed in the exhibition which follows.

Aside from the photograph and title, the antechamber should include the only component of the exhibition specifically suggested by those Wahgi with whom I discussed the exhibition. Their main wish, as earlier noted, was that a contingent of performers should visit the museum to dance and to demonstrate traditional cultural practices, in the way that Hageners had done on their own tour. In the absence of the sponsorship which might make such a visit possible, the only specific proposal they made was that the exhibition should have at its start the large stones, painted posts and cordyline plants which mark the entrance to an area that is in some way special or restricted (as Kinden had marked off my field-base). Kulka Nekinz even painted and presented me with two such posts. In part, I think it was felt that since Wahgi themselves traditionally mark special territory in this way, it was appropriate so to mark the entrance to a Wahgi exhibition. This was reinforced in Kinden's mind by a visit he and I had made a decade earlier to the ethnography exhibitions at the National Museum in the capital, Port Moresby. Kinden had observed near the museum entrance a row of posts or bollards which he had interpreted as similarly delimiting the exhibitions there.

The antechamber leads into a further delimited space (**B** in fig. 52) suitable for providing a conventional introduction to the Wahgi, explaining with the aid of photographs, maps, artefacts and text who they are, where they live and some of the changes they have experienced since their first encounter with the outside world in 1933. Such impersonal, objective presentations are one target of Shanks and Tilley's (1987:97) lively, rhetorical assault on museum practice ('we must oppose professional preservative History with its archaeologist-curator speaking for a monolithic and murdered past'). They suggest that one way in which an exhibition might remain true to the 'fragmentary and discontinuous reality of the past' would be to 'break artifacts from fixed chronological narrative . . . and reassemble them with contemporary artifacts similarly decontextualised'. The combination of grand galleries and exhibition style does sometimes give the impression that museums have access to a unique truth about the past. However, while what Durrans (1992:14) calls the 'privileging effect of the museum habitus' does periodically need to be questioned, the kaleidoscope recommended by Shanks and Tilley may not be the best way of doing so. In order for an oppressive structure of knowledge to be dethroned, it must be enthroned in the first place. My own experience in a museum suggests that the average visitor knows no more about New Guinea than I did myself before I went there. In such circumstances, a synthesis (albeit a provisional one) may be more helpful than precipitate submersion in the vortex Shanks and Tilley propose.

Atypically, the main gallery has a natural anti-clockwise 'visitor-path'.[8] Since the first section offers a clean sweep of wall (**C** in fig. 52), largely free of abutting platforms, it is the obvious area in which to display a selection of Mick Leahy's photographs of the 1933 patrol and subsequent journeyings in the Highlands. One of the existing small wall cases can also be used to exhibit aspects of the photographic technology which went into the making of the pictures, including a borrowed Leica of the type used by Leahy. Because these photographs are so compelling, they require counterpointing by comments from Highlanders themselves on their reactions to the patrol. Visitors to the earlier *Living Arctic* exhibition, which had also used such quotations from Native Americans, repeatedly recorded their approval at the provision of such an 'indigenous voice' – even though the selection of that voice is, of course, the curator's.

At the far end of this section of the gallery, as a further act of counterpointing, it is intended to incorporate a mock-up of a tent similar to that used on the Leahy-Taylor patrol. This will not be merely a gesture in the direction of representing 'us' as well as 'them', for items such as tents and clothing were among those which most intrigued the Highlanders themselves, as they speculated about the intruders' origins and physiology (fig. 53). The nearby 'island' (**D** in fig. 52) makes a convenient point on which to exhibit the spears (fig. 54) which made such an impression on Leahy and Taylor, who insisted that they be left at a distance from the camp. Visitors' access to the tent itself might then be barred with fishing line (represented by the dotted lines in fig. 52), as Leahy and Taylor found they had to segregate their camps from curious

Fig. 53 Girls examine tents at mid-Wahgi airstrip, April 1933; M.J. Leahy Collection, Roll 81 xviii R/30.

Highlanders. In this way, visitors will find themselves temporarily in the position of Highlanders looking in, rather than explorers looking out at Wahgi. This impression might be heightened by mounting life-size photographs of Highlanders on the walls surrounding the tent, so that from a distance visitors to the exhibition are framed by photographs of Highland spectators.

As was described in Chapter 1, Leahy and Taylor partly established themselves through the use of shell wealth, and were soon followed by missionaries who equally deployed shell in their own dealings with Highlanders. It is intended to use the next bay of the gallery (E in fig. 52) to suggest these developments, partly as a necessary background to later stages of the exhibition. A bridewealth banner, mounted with scores of pearl shells, would be the most obvious way to put across the volume of shell which was imported to pay for food and labour. Text, along with photographs of individuals heavily draped in shell ornaments, should help make the point that the 'exotic' appearance of Highlanders at this period was augmented by colonial contact, not depleted by it as the more usual stereotype suggests.

The missionary impact will be suggested through the use of photographs and relevant written material: translations of the New Testament and other religious works into Wahgi, copies of the 'Wordless Gospel' and leaflets enjoining people to 'Pray Before You Vote'. This material on missionisation prefigures the cross, both as erected near the *bolyim* house on the opposite side of the gallery, and as a motif in the netbags in the final section. It is also, of course, relevant in that missionary activity has had specific effects on artefacts: a number of items in the collection were offered for sale because their owners were converting to fundamentalist Christianity, and peacemaking ceremonies are often accompanied by Christian-supervised artefact burning.

Fig. 54 (*Opposite*) Wahgi *kula jimben* spears, with their three barbs above marsupial fur decoration, impressed Leahy and Taylor. 1990 Oc.9.456; L: 316 cm.

The next pre-existing feature in the gallery is the curved raised area (F in fig. 52), originally designed to display costumes from Jerusalem and the central

88

regions of Palestine. This continuous platform lends itself to exhibiting, out of easy touching distance, artefacts relating to a number of linked topics. This area will include a certain amount of reconstruction, but its naturalism will be undercut by juxtaposition with text. The intention is to use the first section to display material culture associated with coffee. Included here will be a hand-powered coffee pulper, the battered kerosene drums into which newly pulped beans are disgorged, coffee beans drying on the vivid blue plastic sheeting which is ubiquitous in Wahgi settlements, and netbags bulked out with harvested coffee 'cherry' (fig. 55).

None of this, of course, is either 'traditional' Wahgi material culture or, perhaps, of great visual interest. But to exclude on these grounds half of the material culture which Wahgi actually use would be to reinforce stereotypes of New Guinea as untouched by cash-cropping, as well as to neglect the quasi-traditional uses to which much of the cash is actually put. There is perhaps also a further reason for incorporating such material. To omit it on the grounds that it is not truly Wahgi would also imply that such peoples, uniquely, cannot change without ceasing to be themselves.

These artefacts associated with coffee production will be exhibited against the side wall of a trade-store which is both the next item encountered on this raised area, and the destination of much coffee income. The adjacent wall of the trade-store, in fact, can also be used to display posters warning of the disease coffee rust, to make the point that Wahgi prosperity is contingent upon this crop and the price paid for it. The store itself (dotted in fig. 52) will be cut away in the front to reveal on its wooden shelving the range of branded foods and other goods with which such a medium-sized store is stocked: *Trukai* ('real food') Rice, different varieties of tinned fish, Ramu sugar, Big Sister pudding, *Muruk* ('cassowary') tobacco, Cambridge cigarettes, *Liklik Wopa* ('little whopper') and Paradise biscuits, Globe dripping, Twisties, Coca-Cola, Fanta, Kurumul Tea, High Mountain Instant Coffee (the only form in which Wahgi drink coffee). Hung at the back will be items of clothing typically on sale: *meri* blouses, the lengths of material known in Pidgin as *laplap*, blankets, caps, sandals, along with axes, bushknives, Chinese-made pots and pans and lanterns. Also on the shelves will be other items of adornment: plastic bottles of face paint, Bigen and Mayflower hairdye, mirrors, beads, combs, the highly-saturated acrylic yarns from which netbags are increasingly made, torches, batteries, kerosene, cassette tapes, soap powder, matches.

Visually, this reconstruction of the trade-store should capture something of the raw colours of such enterprises, as well as the expanding range of goods on sale in the larger ones. Their atmosphere can also be evoked by having the exhibition's soundtrack issue from the store, including tapes of the artists often played in Highlands trade-stores or while travelling on PMVs. Educationally, the trade-store will also be a focus for discussing some of the issues raised thereby: the consequences for subsistence production of cash cropping, the alternatives of spending cash on trade-store goods or using it in ceremonial exchange (not mutually exclusive uses, because trade-store goods can also be given in exchange), and the impact of advertising.

Beer is not generally sold through trade-stores but its presence in Wahgi life can be appropriately incorporated here, through including a stack of cartons of 'South Pacific' empties alongside the far wall of the trade-store. One

Fig. 55 Kekanem Wik operating a pulper to remove the flesh from coffee beans (1990).

of the criticisms made by a Native American visitor to the *Living Arctic* exhibition, referred to earlier, was that the exhibition had been sanitised, with such aspects of life as alcohol omitted. As should be apparent from previous chapters, beer could not be excluded from a contemporary Highlands exhibition, both as a considerable item of expenditure, and as a good which is redeployed within local cultural practices (a point which can be conveyed through accompanying photographs). At the same time, this also needs to be kept in proportion. Accompanying text will make Marshall's (1982:13) point that 'in comparison with the tremendous social disruption and personal destruction alcoholic beverages have wrought among many North American Indian groups, Australian Aborigines and among many other Pacific Islanders . . . Papua New Guinea has experienced quite a smooth passage so far'. Average per capita consumption of beer by residents of Papua New Guinea in the late 1970s was still only one-eighth of that of Australians (Marshall 1982:5).

The most appropriate category of artefact to display directly after trade-store and beer is a selection of the shields discussed in the previous chapter. Spatially, the narrowing of the raised platform at this point suits such two-dimensional objects, while in sequential terms, the trade-store goods and beer are the source of motifs ('Cambridge Cup', 'South Pacific' beer) used in much shield design. The juxtaposition of beer and shields is doubly appropriate in the case of those shields with designs based on 'SP'. As may be recalled, the genesis of this design lay in the perception that 'it was beer alone which had precipitated this fighting'. Also displayed here, and further round the same raised platform, will be other artefacts associated with contemporary fighting: bows and arrows, spears, cassowary plume headdresses, in addition to the technological change embodied in the newly introduced home-made guns.

As with beer, it will be necessary to avoid reinforcing stereotypes of 'tribal warriors', 'naturally' prone to fighting. In addition to including the point from

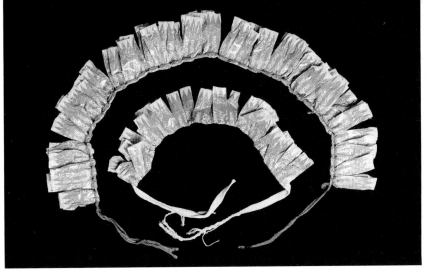

Fig. 56 Headband made from Big Boy bubblegum wrappers whose flame colour closely corresponds to that of one variety of traditional feather headband. 1990 Oc.9.617. L: 82 cm.

the previous chapter, that shield use today partly reflects an attempt to prevent warfare from escalating, this section should include examples of the long bamboo poles on which thousands of pounds' worth of Papua New Guinean currency are arrayed for handing over in battle compensation payments. The accompanying text and large photographs will cover successful peace-making ceremonies, such as that concluded by Komblo with their ancient opponents. Local church people often have a prominent role in such ceremonies, an aspect which will have been prefigured by the earlier section on missions.

Two raised platform areas remain, as do two obvious and self-contained categories of material culture, both of which manifest the processes of continuity within change also exhibited by shield decoration. It is intended to use the first of the platforms (**G** in fig. 52) to display artefacts associated with adornment and the Pig Festival – including a model of the *bolyim* house and *mond* post erected at the Festival's climax. In indigenous terms, there is in fact a measure of appropriateness in positioning material related to the Pig Festival here, facing that on warfare, for in Wahgi thinking the two activities are at once linked but also opposed to each other. On the one hand, Pig Festivals are intended to renew and to assert clan potency in a hostile world. On the other, a pre-requisite for mounting a Pig Festival is a period of peace; furthermore, war-magic houses are said to have been placed out-of-bounds while a Pig Festival was in progress.

As recorded earlier, most Komblo experts felt that though *bolyim* house and *mond* post are intended for public display, it was ritually perilous to make models of them for the collection. Instead, reconstructions will be prepared by the department's creative technical staff. The reconstructed *bolyim* house will, like the majority of those actually made by Komblo clans, be encircled with a decorative ring of beer bottles, with a cross erected nearby: both material evidence of the incorporation of external elements into Wahgi ceremonial.

The same point will emerge from the display on the final platform (**H** in fig. 52), where a dense array of netbags will be exhibited. Those looped from imported acrylic fibres are perhaps the most 'artlike' of the artefacts on display, and they are exhibited at this point in the exhibition partly in an effort to draw visitors down what is at present a *cul de sac* at the end of the gallery. This section too will also incorporate a certain amount of technical information on how netbags are made. Shared techniques have in the past proved to be potent ways in which to bridge cultural distance: exhibitions on textiles and pottery have invariably proven popular, and there is evidence to suggest that the technique of looping is beginning to command international interest (Baker 1985).

'People are intrigued by how ethnographic material is acquired by museums', writes Peirson-Jones (1992:231), in explaining her decision to focus upon the individuals who had collected the ethnographic artefacts recently displayed in the new Gallery 33 at Birmingham Museum and Art Gallery. The way in which visitors are attracted to any kind of case re-arrangement in progress in a museum suggests that they are no less intrigued by how exhibitions come to look as they do. What I have tried to do in this book is to sketch for one exhibition something of these processes of collecting and exhibiting, in addition to providing the more usual information on how the artefacts on display are made, what they are used for, etc. My argument in fact has been that the exhibition is itself a large artefact, whose manufacture merits a measure of the interest usually confined to the component objects included within it. However, I have resisted thus far including any material *on* the exhibition within the exhibition itself. Where the subject of an exhibition is anyway relatively recondite, such mixing of exhibition content, and commentary on that content, risks undermining an exhibition's capacity to convey any message at all. But right at the end of the exhibition, there is in fact vacant wall space (I in fig. 52) where an acknowledgement of the fabricated nature of the exhibition might be made.

This could best be done by including a miscellany of photographs to illustrate the artefacts' passage from field to museum display. The photographs, which would also acknowledge the exhibition's own 'sources', might include: pictures of the artefacts in their Wahgi context; photographs of some of the individuals who use them there, including members of the community at Topkalap under whose care the collection was made; pictures of local accumulators of artefacts, like Kolnga who hoarded shells, and Yap Kupal, founder of the local Cultural Centre; photographs of the making of the crates in which the artefacts were transported, and of Kaipel who both labelled the crates and painted the shields which travelled in them; a picture of the crates leaving for Mt. Hagen in the back of a truck driven by Yimbal (son of the slain Jiruka leader Aipe) who, as I complete this book has just been elected MP for the North Wahgi; an illustration of the artefacts being unpacked upon arrival in London; photographs of the gallery in its previous incarnation exhibiting Palestinian costumes and, if time allows, showing its re-fitting for the present exhibition.

No photographic record remains, however, of the moment which for me illustrated an unavoidable contingency attached to collecting and preserving some artefacts but not others. In the museum's repository, the process of unpacking the crates in which the collection had travelled was complete. The crates' contents, now safely swaddled in tissue paper, awaited fumigation, conservation, registration and careful storage as Wahgi artefacts. Meanwhile, other Wahgi artefacts – the crates themselves, no less carefully made by Michael Du, painted by Zacharias and labelled by Kaipel the sign-writer – awaited disposal.

Notes

INTRODUCTION

1 However, the exhibition itself focuses upon the Wahgi more generally, not Komblo in particular. Komblo are simply the lens used in this book to explore Wahgi history more broadly.

2 From another point of view, of course, the urgency is increased, in order to document all the changing material forms through which the culture in question expresses itself.

3 See here in particular Anderson's (1990) notion of 'engagement', and his analysis of Australian Aboriginal artefacts as 'social currency' in the relationship between Aboriginal communities and museums.

CHAPTER 1

1 See Weiner (1991) for another example of pervasive directionality encoded in language.

2 Both these products are traditional exports from the Kopn (Jimi Valley) area.

3 A term I borrow from Meigs (1984:13).

4 Here I have relied heavily on Connolly and Anderson's (1987) account, itself entitled *First Contact*.

5 Patrol Report 1933a:xvi. 'Gardnor' is Kar Nol, 'Kar River'.

6 In fact Kolip's declaration is intentionally ironic; in reality, he too is 'born of a Komblo woman'. In speaking this way, he was announcing his intention of contravening custom by taking sides against his 'source people'.

7 The only significant exception was some continued intermarriage with the Sekaka subgroup of Waplka. It should be noted that data for the earliest periods shown in fig. 7 is less complete, reflecting amongst other factors a tendency to forget those marriages which did not produce sons.

8 It is from this period that we have our first reliable fix for Komblo's population, recorded as 562. Census figures document the subsequent increase as follows: 581 in 1955, 605 in 1957, 663 in 1962, 708 in 1965, 753 in 1967/8, 860 in 1980, 1,200 in 1990.

9 Formerly, Wahgi obtained almost all shells from Hagen groups to their west, hence 'up-river'. Only cowrie shells travelled from 'down-river up'.

10 The thinking is that Kekanem brides marrying into the killer's subclan will be distinguished by their infertility or poor appearance compared with those marrying into other Anzkanem subclans.

11 In this instance, what was assessed was the relative fertility of Anzkanem girls who had married into the different Kekanem subclans.

12 Although Reay does also note that South Wall Wahgi believed that the mission's determination to exorcise war magic houses made their dismantling inevitable (the mid-1960s was perhaps a peak of mission influence).

13 Comments by Labour Inspector Dalziel on Minj Patrol Report no. 7, 1965/66.

14 Patrol Report no. 8, 1965/6.

15 Patrol Report no. 8, 1965/6.

16 Patrol Report no. 5a, 1969/70.

17 Patrol Report no. 7, 1969/70 for South Wahgi.

18 Gilma lived across the Binz and Mambel rivers in the Jimi Valley. Though it is Gilma's own drinking which is recalled in this mourning song, it was actually another's inebriation which killed him. Unknown to Gilma, his open-backed vehicle had been boarded by a drunken passenger who fell to his death trying to catch his hat when it was swept off by the wind. Gilma was then killed by the dead man's vengeful clansmen when they broke in to Banz police station where Gilma had sought refuge.

19 See O'Hanlon 1989: ch.6 for a fuller account.

20 An illustration of contemporary Highlands warfare appears in Connolly and Anderson's recent film *Black Harvest*.

21 *Post Courier*, 19 September 1990.

22 Patrol Report no. 1, 1957/8.

CHAPTER 2

1 As may also occur in the West; see in particular Carrier (1992) on the perils of constructing uncritical antitheses.

2 See also Price and Price (1992), whose own account of a collecting trip appears just as this book is going to press.

3 On the programme *01 for London*, Thames TV, 31 May 1990.

4 See also Clark (1991).

5 Although Kenzamb did not classify the shell in this way, Wahgi sometimes refer to artefacts with such links to the past as 'path things' (*kol wal*).

6 The authority on Wahgi shields is John Muke, himself a native Wahgi speaker who, as part of his postgraduate work at Cambridge, made a study of shield-use near Minj in the southeast corner of the Wahgi. My own data derives mainly from the shields used by North Wall groups in fighting in 1989, though I also made a number of visits to the Minj area where I saw shields in use in 1986. I am most grateful to John Muke for discussing his findings with me.

7 Known as 'great *tapi*' or '*tapi* mother' (*tapi mam*).

8 Some shields also have a design in punctuate inscribed on them.

9 Though in practice the lettering would not often have been visible at any great distance.

10 I am grateful to Andrew Strathern for stimulating this train of thought.

11 See also Jerry Leach's excellent film *Trobriand Cricket* for a much earlier account both of the incorporation of commodities into local art, and for an example of the interplay of warfare and sport.

12 Equally, the tools of netbag production have changed; pandanus stitch-gauges have been replaced by plastic strapping, and needles are now often made from umbrella spokes rather than flying-fox bone.

13 Cf also Strathern 1979b:124-5.

14 A similar attitude informs people's accounts today of their reactions to the Leahy-Taylor patrol.

CHAPTER 3

1 Notable examples of this expanding literature include Karp and Lavine (1991), Karp *et al* (1992), Pearce (1992) and the new *Journal of the History of Collections*.

2 Recent exceptions include Herle 1990, Sant Cassia 1992 and, earlier, van Gulik *et al* 1980.

3 Some of these points, and others, were made by the exhibition's curator in his response to the review (Shelton 1988).

4 This argument is complicated by the fact that objects in museum storage may actually be more rather than less accessible than those stored in indigenous contexts. Some museums have 'open storage' policies; others readily give access to objects not currently on display (as in fact does the Museum of Mankind).

5 John Muke's photographs of the same shield in use during warfare the previous year confirm that the re-painted design is identical to the original (personal communication).

6 One exception is the unique Moriarty collection on display in the Art Gallery of New South Wales in Sydney.

7 The more usual practice for the museum's Design Office would be for the designer to produce a break-down of the curator's exhibition-brief, and to suggest on that basis an effective layout for conveying the exhibition's messages.

8 More usually, British Museum exhibitions are given a clockwise visitor-path, since designers feel that it is easier for visitors to circulate in the same left to right direction as they read the lines of text on exhibition information panels.

Bibliography

01 for London. Thames Television tx 31 May 1990.

Anderson, C. 1990 'The economics of sacred art: the uses of a secret collection in the South Australian Museum', in *Bulletin of the Conference of Museum Anthropologists*, 23, 31-42.

Baker, S. 1985 *Make your own bilum*. Brisbane: Boolarong Publications.

Baxandall, M. 1991 'Exhibiting intention: some preconditions of the visual display of culturally purposeful objects', in Karp and Lavine (eds.).

Beard, M., and Henderson, J. 1991 'Labels and slanders', *New Statesman*, issue of 20 and 27 December.

Bouquet, M. 1991 'On two-way translation', *Man* n.s. 26, 162-3.

Brookfield, H.C., and Brown, P. 1963 *Struggle for land*. Melbourne: Oxford University Press.

Bruce, R.G. 1992 *The study of law and order in Papua New Guinea: social deviance and identity among the Kuma-Kondika of the South Wahgi*. Cambridge University Ph.D. thesis.

Burton, J. 1983 'A dysentery epidemic in New Guinea and its mortality', *Journal of Pacific History*, 18, 236-61.

Burton, J. 1984 *Axe makers of the Wahgi*. Australian National University: Ph.D thesis.

Burton, J. 1991 'The Romunga *Haus Tumbuna*, Western Highlands Province, PNG', in *Museums and cultural centres in the Pacific*, eds S.M. Eoe and P. Swadling. Port Moresby: Papua New Guinea National Museum.

Carrier, J.G. 1992 'Occidentalism: the world turned upside-down', *American Ethnologist* 19, 195-212.

Clark, J. 1991 'Pearlshell symbolism in Papua New Guinea, with particular reference to the Wiru people of Southern Highlands Province'. *Oceania* 61, 309-340.

Clifford, J. 1985 'Objects and selves — an afterword', in *Objects and others: essays on museums and material culture*, ed. G. Stocking. Madison: University of Wisconsin Press.

Clifford, J. 1988 *The Predicament of culture: twentieth-century ethnography, literature, and art*. Cambridge: Harvard University Press.

Connolly, B., and Anderson, R. 1987 *First contact*. New York: Viking Penguin.

Connolly, B., and Anderson, R. 1992 *Black Harvest* (film) Arundel Productions, Australia.

Corrigan, B. (see: Patrol Report No 3 of 1952/3).

Cruikshank, J. 1992 'Oral tradition and material culture: multiplying meanings of "words" and "things"', *Anthropology Today* 8, (3), 5-9.

Durrans, B. 1988 'The future of the other: changing cultures on display in ethnographic museums', in *The museum time machine: putting cultures on display*, ed. R. Lumley. London: Routledge.

Durrans, B. 1992 'Behind the scenes: museums and selective criticism', *Anthropology Today* 8, (4), 11-15.

Frankel, S. 1986 *The Huli response to illness*. Cambridge University Press.

Good, K. 1979 'The formation of the peasantry', in *Development and dependency: the political economy of Papua New Guinea*, eds A. Amarshi, K. Good, and R. Mortimer. Oxford University Press.

Gordon, R.J., and Meggitt, M.J. 1985 *Law and order in the New Guinea Highlands*. Hanover: University Press of New England.

Hannerz, U. 1991 'Scenarios for peripheral cultures', in *Culture, globalization and the world-system*, ed. A.D. King. London: Macmillan.

Healey, C. 1990 *Maring hunters and traders: production and exchange in the Papua New Guinea Highlands*. Berkeley: University of California Press.

Heaney, W. 1982 'The changing role of bird of paradise plumes in bridewealth in the Wahgi Valley', in *Traditional conservation in P.N.G.: implications for today*, eds L. Morauta, J. Pernetta and W. Heaney. Port Moresby: IASER monograph, No. 16.

Herle, A. 1990 'Medium and message in an anthropological exhibit: curating "The Nagas"', *Society for Visual Anthropology Review*, 6, (2), 55-61.

Hughes, I. 1978 'Good money and bad: inflation and devaluation in the colonial process', *Mankind* 11, 308-18.

Journal of the History of Collections, 1989-cont. Oxford University Press.

Kaeppler, A.L. 1992 '*Ali'i* and *Maka'ainana*: the representation of Hawaiians in museums at home and abroad', in Karp, Kreamer, and Lavine (eds).

Karp, I., and Lavine, S.D. 1991 (eds) *Exhibiting cultures: the poetics and politics of museum display*. Washington: Smithsonian Institution Press.

Karp, I, Kreamer, C.M. and Lavine, S.D. 1992 (eds) *Museums and communities: the politics of public culture*. Washington: Smithsonian Institution Press.

Knauft, B.M. 1990 'Melanesian warfare: a theoretical history', *Oceania* 60, 250-311.

Kondwal, A., and Trompf, G. 1982 'The epic of the Komblo, Western Highlands Province', *Oral History* 10, (1), 88-116.

Leach, J. 1973 *Trobriand cricket: an ingenious response to colonialism*. University of California Extension Media Center.

Leahy, M., and Crane, M. 1937 *The land that time forgot*. London: Hurst and Blackett.

Lederman, R. 1986 'The return of redwoman: field work in Highland New Guinea', in *Women in the field*, ed. P. Golde. Berkeley: University of California Press.

Lowman, C. 1973 *Displays of power: art and war among the Marings of New Guinea*. New York: Museum of Primitive Art, Studies, 6.

Luzbetak, L.J. 1958 'The Middle Wahgi culture', *Anthropos 53*, 51-87.

MacKenzie, M.A. 1991 *Androgynous objects: string bags and gender in central New Guinea*. Chur: Harwood Academic Publishers.

Marshall, M. 1982 Introduction to *Through a glass darkly: beer and modernization in Papua New Guinea*, ed. M. Marshall. Boroko: IASER monograph, No. 18.

Mead, S.M. 1983 'Indigenous models of museums in Oceania' *Museum, 138*, 98-101.

Meggitt, M.J. 1965 *The lineage system of the Mae-Enga of New Guinea*. Edinburgh: Oliver and Boyd.

Meigs, A.S. 1984 *Food, sex, and pollution: a New Guinea religion*. New Brunswick: Rutgers University Press.

Mell, M.Y. 1988 *The Handbook of the Western Highlands Province and its Government*. Port Moresby: Mell Productions and Publishing Agents.

Mennis, M.R. 1982 *Hagen saga: the story of Father William Ross*. Boroko: Institute of Papua New Guinea Studies.

Nengo, P. 1991 *Tinpis run* (film). J.B.A. Productions, France/Belgium/P.N.G.

Nunley, J.W. 1987 *Moving with the face of the devil: art and politics in urban West Africa*. Urbana: University of Illinois Press.

O'Hanlon, M. 1989 *Reading the skin: adornment, display and society among the Wahgi*. London: British Museum Publications.

Parry, J., and Bloch, M. 1989 Introduction to *Money and the morality of exchange*. Cambridge University Press.

Patrol Reports:
1933a Mount Hagen Patrol Report, 19 Feb. 1934 (Australian Archives A7034, Item 56). Taylor, J.L.
1933b Preliminary Report [on Mount Hagen patrol], 30 Aug. 1933 (Australian Archives A7034, Item 56). Taylor, J.L.
1952/53 no. 3 Corrigan, B.
1957/58 no. 1 Blaikie, R.W.
1959/60 no. 1 Richardson, H.A.
1965/66 no. 7 Walshe, P.J.
1965/66 no. 8 Patrol Officer Wallace
1966/67 no. 1 Moore, J.M.
1969/70 no. 5a Young, F.J.
1969/70 no. 7 Ziesing, P.R.

Pearce, S.M. 1992 *Museum objects and collections: a cultural study*. Leicester University Press.

Peirson-Jones, J.P. 1992 'The colonial legacy and the community: the Gallery 33 project', in Karp, Kreamer and Lavine (eds).

Platt, T. 1987 'Museums, tourism and the devil at Burlington Gardens', *Anthropology Today 3*, (4), 13-16.

Price, R., and S. 1992 *Equatoria*. New York and London: Routledge.

Reay, M.O. 1971 'Structural co-variants of land shortage among patrilineal peoples', in *Politics in New Guinea*, eds R.M. Berndt and P. Lawrence. Nedlands: University of Western Australia Press.

Reay, M.O. 1982 'Abstinence, excess and opportunity: Minj, 1963-1980' in Marshall (ed.).

Sahlins, M. 1985 *Islands of history*. Chicago: University of Chicago Press.

Sant Cassia, P. 1992 'Ways of Displaying', *Museums Journal 92*, (1), 28-31.

Schieffelin, E.L. 1991 Introduction to *Like people you see in a dream: first contact in six Papuan societies*, eds E.L. Schieffelin and R. Crittenden. Stanford University Press.

Shanks, M., and Tilley, C. 1987 *Re-Constructing archaeology: theory and practice*. Cambridge University Press.

Shelton, A. 1988 'Platt's review of "Bolivian Worlds"', letter to the Editor *Anthropology Today 4*, (3), 27-8.

Shipton, P. 1989 *Bitter money: cultural economy and some African meanings of forbidden commodities*. American Ethnological Society Monograph Series, 1.

Sillitoe, P. 1978 'Big men and war in New Guinea', *Man* n.s. *13*, 252-271.

Sillitoe, P. 1980 'The art of war: Wola shield designs', *Man* n.s. *15*, 483-501.

Sillitoe, P. 1988 *Made in Niugini: technology in the Highlands of Papua New Guinea*. London: British Museum Publications.

Stewart, S. 1984 *On longing: narratives of the miniature, the gigantic, the souvenir, the collection*. Baltimore: Johns Hopkins University Press.

Strathern, A.J. 1971 'Cargo and inflation in Mount Hagen', *Oceania 41*, 255-65.

Strathern, A.J. 1977 'Contemporary warfare in the New Guinea Highlands: revival or breakdown?', *Yagl-ambu 4*, 135-146.

Strathern, A.J. 1979a 'Gender, ideology and money in Mount Hagen', *Man* n.s. *14*, 530-548.

Strathern, A.J. 1979b *Ongka: a self-account by a New Guinea big-man*. London: Duckworth.

Strathern, A.J. 1981 '"Noman": representations of identity in Mount Hagen', in *The structure of folk models*, eds L. Holy and M. Stuchlik. London: Academic Press.

Strathern, A.J. 1984 *A line of power*. London: Tavistock.

Strathern, A.J. 1985 '"A line of boys": Melpa dance as a symbol of maturation', in *Society and the dance*, ed. P. Spencer. Cambridge University Press.

Strathern, A.J. 1992 'Let the bow go down', in *War in the tribal zone: expanding States and indigenous warfare*, eds R.B. Ferguson and N.L. Whitehead. Santa Fe: School of American Research Press.

Taylor, J.L. (see: Patrol Reports 1933)

Thomas, N. 1991 *Entangled objects: exchange, material culture, and colonialism in the Pacific*. Cambridge: Harvard University Press.

Tinpis run: see Nengo

Trompf (see Kondwal and)

van Beek, G. 1990 'The rites of things: a critical view of museums, objects, and metaphors', *Etnofoor 3*, (1), 26-44.

van Gulik, W.R., van der Straaten, H.S., and van Wengen, G.D. eds 1980 *From field-case to show-case: research, acquisition and presentation in the Rijksmuseum voor Volkenkunde (National Museum of Ethnology), Leiden*. Amsterdam: J.C. Gieben.

Warry, W. 1982 '*Bia* and *bisnis*: the use of beer in Chuave ceremonies', in Marshall (ed.).

Weiner, J.F. 1991 *The empty place: poetry, space and being among the Foi of Papua New Guinea*. Bloomington: Indiana University Press.

Wilson, D.M. 1989 *The British Museum: purpose and politics*. London: British Museum Publications.

95

Index